A Treasury
of Iqbal

THE TREASURY SERIES IN
ISLAMIC THOUGHT AND CIVILISATION

I.   *A Treasury of Ḥadīth*, Ibn Daqīq al-ʿĪd

II. *A Treasury of al-Ghazālī*, Mustafa Abu Sway

III. *A Treasury of Sacred Maxims*, Dr. Shahrul Hussain

IV. *A Treasury of Ibn Taymiyyah*, Mustapha Sheikh

V.   *A Treasury of Rūmī*, Dr. Muhammad Isa Waley

VI. *A Treasury of Iqbal*, Abdur Rashid Siddiqui

VII. *A Treasury of Aishah*, Sofia Rehman
     (Forthcoming)

Abdur Rashid Siddiqui

❊ ❊ ❊

كنوز من أقبال

A Treasury
of Iqbal

جوانوں کو سوزِ جگر بخش دے

مرا عشق ، میری نظر بخش دے

(بالِ جبریل، ص ۱۲۸)

Endow the Young with Fervent Soul;
Grant them my Vision, my Passion

KUBE
PUBLISHING

A Treasury of Iqbal

First published in England by
Kube Publishing Ltd
Markfield Conference Centre
Ratby Lane, Markfield
Leicestershire LE67 9SY
United Kingdom

TEL +44 (0)1530 249230
FAX +44 (0)1530 249656

WEBSITE www.kubepublishing.com
EMAIL info@kubepublishing.com

CIP data for this book is available from the British Library.

ISBN 978-1-84774-165-3 casebound
ISBN 978-1-84774-166-0 ebook

Cover design by: Inspiral Design
Book design by: Imtiaze Ahmed
Arabic & English typesetting by: nqaddoura@hotmail.com
Printed by: Elma Basim, Turkey

For
Maya and Kyan

Transliteration Table

Arabic Consonants

Initial, unexpressed medial and final: ʾ ʿ

ا	a	د	d	ض	ḍ	ك	k
ب	b	ذ	dh	ط	ṭ	ل	l
ت	t	ر	r	ظ	ẓ	م	m
ث	th	ز	z	ع	ʿ	ن	n
ج	j	س	s	غ	gh	هـ	h
ح	ḥ	ش	sh	ف	f	و	w
خ	kh	ص	ṣ	ق	q	ي	y

with a *shaddah*, both medial and final consonants are doubled.

Vowels, diphthongs, etc.

Short:　　　　 ﹷ a　　 ﹻ i　　 ﹹ u

Long:　　　　 ﹷـا ā　　 ﹻـي ī　　 ﹹـو ū

Diphthongs:　　　　　 ﹷـو aw
　　　　　　　　　　 ﹷـى ay

Contents

Acknowledgements   IX
Introduction   1

1. God   7
2. God and Man   12
3. The Universe   18
4. Time and Space   23
5. Life   28
6. Death and Immortality of Soul   33
7. Satan   37
8. Clash of Good and Evil   41
9. Predestination   54
10. Reason and Love   49
11. The Qur'ān   53
12. The Prophet (peace be upon him)   57
13. The Perfect Man   62
14. Shāhīn (The Eagle)   66
15. Unity of the Ummah   71
16. Causes of the Downfall of Muslims   75
17. Sufism   80

18. The Individual and Society 85
19. Ijtihād 89
20. Khūdī (Self-Respect, Ego) 93
21. Bikhūdī 98
22. Faqr 103
23. Conviction 107
24. Education 111
25. Science 116
26. Fine Art 120
27. Women 124
28. Youth 129
29. Children 134
30. Western Civilization 138
31. Political System 142
32. Nationalism 146
33. Democracy 151
34. Capitalism 155
35. Marxism 159
36. Rūmī 164
37. Goethe 169
38. Nietzsche 173
39. Vision of Pakistan 177
40. Zindah Rūd 182

Glossary of Terms 194
Bibliography 200

Acknowledgments

❀ ❀ ❀

G rateful thanks to Allah *Subhanahu wa Ta'ala* Who enabled me to write *A Treasury of Iqbal*. This was truly for me a labour of love as it provided me the opportunity to read Iqbal again and become imbued in his divinely inspired poetry. Hence, my thanks to Kube Publishing for asking me to undertake this work. In the last hundred years a great deal has been written in multiple languages on Iqbal and his legacy, so much so that it is impossible to consult them all. In this respect I am grateful to my very dear brother Khurshid Ahmad to provide me with some invaluable works from his library and also Islamic Foundation Markfield Library who lent me many books on Iqbal. Without their help I would not have been able to do justice to this task.

Prof. Salman Nadvi was a superb source of inspiration who guided me throughout with his valuable advice by meticulously going through my manuscript. He also provided many references on Iqbal. He rightly pointed out the difficulty in translating the Islamic term used by Iqbal. To provide the equivalent terms in English has been a challenge. I have provided a Glossary and tried to explain essential terminology and historical illusions that occur in

Iqbal's poetry. I must admit that I may not always be successful in conveying the precise meanings. I am also indebted to Prof. Abdur Raheem Kidwai for his encouragement and advice.

The transcribing of the Urdu and Persian poems is a difficult task and this could not have been done without the help of Br. Salim Mansur Khalid. Br. Sadiq Khokar provided him with the references which were then transcribed and typeset, the latter by Br. Naiem Qaddoura. May Allah reward all who helped in producing this book.

Introduction

※ ※ ※

Mohammad Iqbal is one of the most illustrious poet-philosophers of Islam as well as one of the key political figures who flourished in the Indo-Pakistan sub-continent during the last century. He was born on 9 November 1877 in Sialkot, Punjab then part of British India. His family hailed from Kashmir. His grandfather Sheikh Rafīq moved from Kashmir to Sialkot. His father, Sheikh Nūr Muḥammad, was an accomplished tailor and embroider who kept the company of Sufis and acquired mystic knowledge. His mother Imām Bībī was also deeply religious.

Iqbal started his early education in a *Maktab* (elementary madrasah) in Sialkot and after finishing that he was fortunate to have the benefit of being taught by a very accomplished teacher, Sayyid Mīr Ḥasan (1844–1929) an eminent scholar of Islamic studies as well as Arabic and Persian literature. He persuaded Iqbal's father to have his son admitted to Sialkot's Scotch Mission College (now Murray College) for further education. After completing the Intermediate course at College, Iqbal joined the Government College in Lahore. Here Iqbal had the good fortune to study under Professor T.W. Arnold (1864–1930) who was a British orientalist and historian of Islamic art. He taught at the Muhammadan Anglo-Oriental College (now Aligarh Muslim University) and later joined the Government College in Lahore. Iqbal's talents flourished under his stewardship. It stirred in him the urge to acquire more education and expand his horizons. Iqbal developed a close relationship with his teacher and was much influenced by him. Intellectually Iqbal blossomed at college where he studied liberal arts and obtained both Bachelors and Masters Degrees. During this period he also attended the Oriental College, Lahore to complete his education of Arabic. After graduating Iqbal secured the job of Reader of Arabic at the University's Oriental College.

Iqbal started composing poetry at an early age under the guidance of Mīr Ḥassan. Like all beginners he needed the help of an *ustād* – a teacher. He chose Nawāb Mirzā Khān Dāgh (1831–1905), a renowned poet, as his mentor. At that time, Iqbal was already well known through his Urdu poetry and his interest in world literature. His poetry generated much interest. He also regularly participated in *Mushā'aras* (poetry recital gatherings).

In 1892 his parents married him to Karīm Bibī. Three children were born from this marriage: Mi'rāj Begum, Āftāb Iqbāl and the third child died in infancy. This was not a happy marriage, and the couple separated after two decades of living together.

When Prof. Arnold returned to England in 1904 he encouraged Iqbal to acquire a higher education in

Europe. In 1905, he went to England and enrolled as an undergraduate at Trinity College, Cambridge studying philosophy. He also started his legal studies at Lincoln's Inn as well as completing his doctoral dissertation, entitled "*The Development of Metaphysics in Persia*" at the University of Munich. Thus, during his three years' stay in Europe Iqbal obtained a BA degree from Cambridge, qualification as a barrister from Lincoln's Inn in London and award of a PhD from Munich University, Germany.

In Europe he met great scholars like John McTaggart, the philosopher; R. Nicholson and E. G. Browne, both scholars of Persian literature. Later on Prof. Nicholson translated Iqbal's *Asrār-i-Khūdī* into English, and as a consequence introduced him to the Western audience.

In 1908 Iqbal returned to India and started practising at the Bar. In 1909 he married again, this time to Sardar Begun from a respectable Kashmiri family. He had a son Javed and a daughter Munirah. Iqbal was a prolific writer in Urdu, Persian and English. After returning from Europe he started writing poetry in Persian so that his message could reach a wider Muslim audience as well as orientalists in Europe. His poems were translated into English by Prof. Nicholson and Arthur J. Arberry. In 1922 the British Government in recognition of his scholarship awarded him a knighthood.

In addition to writing poetry, Iqbal's major work in English was his thesis mentioned earlier. He also gave a series of lectures at the invitation of the Madras (now known as Chennai) Muslim Educational Association of Southern India in 1929 and further lectures were given in other Indian cities. These were later published as *The Reconstruction of Religious thought in Islam*. These philosophical lectures are the *magnum opus* of Iqbal's prose works. In this Iqbal argued that there was no finality in philosophical thought and it was a pity that Muslim religious thought had become stagnant and for the last five hundred years had been practically stationary. Thus, he argued for reviving the concept of *ijtihād* (Juridical Reasoning based on the Qur'ān and the Sunnah). For this purpose a new mechanism could be set up with the help of well-qualified 'ulamā' and lawyers who would systematically revise the *fiqh* rulings.

Iqbal also started taking an active part in politics and joined the All India Muslim League. He contested an election and became a member of the Punjab Legislative Assembly. His historic address in 1930 at Allahabad to the All India Muslim League was arguably the call to establish a separate Muslim homeland. He attended two Round-Table Conferences in England in 1931 and 1932 convened by the British Government on the future of India. He spent 1933 in Afghanistan at the invitation of King Nādir Shāh as an advisor on education. With the help of other scholars he presented a planning document for modernizing the education system in that country.

On studying Iqbal's life and works one is impressed by his sheer brilliance and the underlying fervor of his faith. It was his unflinching faith which acted as an anchor and kept him within the religious bounds despite living in permissive Western countries. His love of the Prophet (peace be upon him) and the Qur'ān permeated profusely throughout his writings. As he had developed the concept of *Khūdī* (self-realization and self-respect) he himself became its embodiment. His life was an example of living with contentment and persevering integrity, self-respect and self-confidence against all odds. His early morning prayers and sincere devotions enlightened his insight which was further influenced by his passionate love for Rūmī's *Mathnawī.*

> Your heart and mind spellbound by
> the West;
> In Rūmī's burning zeal is a cure and rest.
> By his blessings my vision shines and glows
> By his blessings mighty Oxus too is in my
> pitcher flows.[1]

Human beings are the centre-piece in Iqbal's poetry and thought, in keeping with the ethos of the Qur'ān. Iqbal's major contribution lies in presenting the vision of Humanity in relation to God in a manner that makes the finite honourable and lovable in the shadow of the Infinite. Humanity's role is that of vicegerency and stewardship, striving to realize the Divine Will within the human context, in space and time.

Iqbal was a versatile genius. Many aspects of his personality shine. His elegant style and the beauty of his superb artistic presentations captivate the heart. One is amazed at the wide-ranging coverage of his topics with his depth of thought. He was equally at home with his philosophical discourses as well as his political discussions. One may consider him as a great poet, a brilliant thinker and philosopher as well as a seasoned politician but above all he was a pioneer of the Renaissance of Islam in the twentieth century. This bestows on him the greatest honour.

From 1934 onwards his health began to decline and he died on 21 April 1938. He was deeply mourned by Muslims and non-Muslims alike. His funeral prayers were attended by more than a hundred thousand people. His simple tomb in front of the Grand Bādshāhī Mosque in Lahore reflects his deep attachment to Islam. In 1947 his dream of an independent Muslim nation materialized in the form of Pakistan and he is considered to be the founding father of that nation.

God

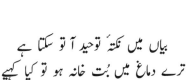

بیاں میں نکتۂ توحید آ تو سکتا ہے
ترے دماغ میں بُت خانہ ہو تو کیا کہیے

(ضربِ کلیم، ص ۶۶)

Subtlety of *Tawḥīd* can be explained,
But what, if your mind is a house of idols.[2]

*I*qbal, as a Muslim believed in One God. As a philosopher he had his own concept of God. According to him, God is the Ultimate Ego and its infinity "consists in infinite inner possibilities of His creative activity of which the universe, as known to us, is only partial expression. In one word God's infinity is intensive, not extensive...The other important elements in the Qur'anic conception of God, from purely intellectual point of view, are Creativeness, Knowledge, Omnipotence and Eternity."[3] For him the existence of God is manifested all around us. There are innumerable signs scattered all around the universe both in the heavens and the earth: their creation and their order and arrangement are enough to convince one of the existence of a Creator. Then again if one ponders over their own creation and the sublime beauty and proportionality of their different body parts they all lead one to "the Most High, Who created all things and fashioned them in good proportion". (87: 1–2)

> Look not at the garden of existence like a stranger
> It is worth looking at, so look at it repeatedly.
> If your eyes are opened for longing to see
> Then the beloved's footprint is in every pathway.[4]

Thus, by intensive reflection and deep observation the Qur'ān wants to awaken our consciousness of the Creator – as this universe is His manifestation.

Iqbal considered the classical arguments of God's existence but concluded that Kant was right that none of these were conclusive. He also doubted the validity of Kant's moral argument for the existence of God. He believed God's existence can only be established by a totality of experience and agreed with al-Fārābī and other Muslim thinkers who maintained that God Himself is the proof of all beings, and therefore needs no proof for His existence.

هر چیز ہے محوِ خود نمائی

ہر ذرّہ شہیدِ کبریائی

اِک تُو ہے کہ حق ہے اس جہاں میں

باقی ہے نُمودِ سیمیائی

ہیں عقدہ کُشا یہ خارِ صحرا

کم کر گلّہِ برہنہ پائی

(بالِ جبریل، ص۵۹)

Everything is bent on self-revelation,
Every particle is dying for expansion to divinity!
You are the world's sole truth, all else
Illusion, sorcery and wizardry.
Success lies beyond these thorns of desert
Complain not if bare feet bleed.[5]

Cognizance of God could not be acquired unless
one has self-knowledge. Unless a person tries to
understand their own natural desires and instincts they
will remain ignorant of the secrets of the Universe's
Creator. It is one's own *Khūdī* (self-realization) that
unveils *Khudā* (God):

Its appearance is your appearance
Your appearance is His appearance.
You expose God
And God will expose you.

For those who doubt the existence of God, Iqbal was
more sarcastic by denying their existence. Unless
they can prove the reality of their own existence they
could not understand the Ultimate Reality.

> In your view there is no proof of God's existence.
> In my view there is no proof of your existence.
> What is existence? The manifestation of the
> essence of *khūdī*
> You should worry about yourself as your essence
> is still obscure.[6]

The principle of *Tawḥīd* (Oneness of God) is the
essence of the Universe as well as a person's spiritual
life. The plurality which is all around us cannot be
explained without the unifying force which is keeping
everything in order. Iqbal in his poem *Lā ilāha illā
Allāh* (*There is no deity but Allah*) starts with a
person's own *khūdī* (self-realization) and states that
they will only comprehend it in the context of the
concept and belief in *Tawḥīd*; the same applies to
the rest of the universe. In modern times, human
beings have instead of stone idols, carved other idols
and these have to be smashed as well.

خودی کا سِرّ نہاں لَا اِلہَ اِلَّا اللہ
خودی ہے تیغ فَساں لَا اِلہَ اِلَّا اللہ

یہ دور اپنے براہیم کی تلاش میں ہے
صنم کدہ ہے جہاں ، لَا اِلہَ اِلَّا اللہ

کیا ہے تُو نے متاعِ غرور کا سودا

فریبِ سود و زیاں ، لَا اِلٰہَ اِلَّا اللہ

یہ مال و دولتِ دُنیا ، یہ رشتہ و پیوند

بتانِ وہم و گماں ، لَا اِلٰہَ اِلَّا اللہ

(ضربِ کلیم، ۷۷/۴/۱۵)

The hidden secret of *khūdī* is
Lā ilāha illā Allāh.
Khūdī is a sword and its sharpness is
Lā ilāha illā Allāh.
This age is still searching for its Ibrāhīm.
The world is a temple of idols
Lā ilāha illā Allāh.
The worldly possessions and wealth and
these relations and friends
These are imaginary and shadowy idols.
Lā ilāha illā Allāh.[7]

Throughout Iqbal's poetry there is forceful stress on *Tawḥīd* and he has explained the significance of this article of faith repeatedly in captivating ways.

The revolving point of the universe is *Lā ilāha.*
The concluding end of the universe is *Lā ilāha.*
Lā and *illāha* are the scrutiny of the universe.
Lā and *illāha* are the opening door of the universe.
Until you understand the significance of *Lā ilāha.*
You cannot defeat the forces of evil.

2

God and Man

O Waiting Reality! Reveal Thyself in a
figurative dress
A thousand prostrations are waiting to be
bestowed from my humble forehead.[8]

or many people the only relationship they have with
God is through Prayer and supplication.

For Iqbal the ritual worship constitutes a believer's
passive relationship with their Creator. Iqbal wants
to engage in constant dialogue and seeks to unravel
the mysteries of the universe. Treating God as a
friend, a term which the Qur'ān has used for God,
Iqbal presents to Him problems he finds puzzling and
frustrating. He comments on the human condition he
finds depressing. Thus he holds intimate conversation
with God.

Shikwah (*The Complaint*) by far became the most
controversial, in it Iqbal audaciously addressed the

Almighty apparently in a manner which shook pious Muslims. In this poem he extols the tremendous role Muslims have played for centuries by preaching Islam in the four corners of the world. However, he boldly complains to God that He has let down Muslims and now they are living in subjugation and disgrace.

Shikwah was published in 1909 and instantly became very popular as well as controversial. By 1913 the furore had died down, and Iqbal composed an equally eloquent reply to the complaint from God (*Jawāb-i-Shikwah*). In this respect, shortcomings of Muslims, their internal strife, weakness of their faith, love of material gains and abandoning of their mission were mentioned by God as the causes for their downfall.

In another rather dramatic poem, *A Dialogue between God and Man*, where the Creator and His creation come face to face to present their cases. This time it is God who accuses human beings of misusing their intelligence and mistreating the resources provided to them. They divided humanity on the basis of their country of origin, colour and race. Instead of appreciating natural beauty, human beings violated the freedom of other creatures.

In turn, the response of human beings was that they have contributed towards nurturing and embellishing the crude natural environment and beautifying it. They have illuminated the dark nights by creating lamps and transformed the barren land into meadows

and gardens as well as turning harmful ingredients
into delicious food.

As it is a short poem it is quoted below:

جہاں را ز یک آب و گِل آفریدم
تو ایران و تاتار و زنگ آفریدی

من از خاک پولادِ ناب آفریدم
تو شمشیر و تیر و تفنگ آفریدی

تبر آفریدی نہالِ چمن را
قفس ساختی طائرِ نغمہ زن را

تو شب آفریدی چراغ آفریدم
سفال آفریدی ایاغ آفریدم

بیابان و کہسار و راغ آفریدی
خیابان و گلزار و باغ آفریدم

من آنم کہ از سنگ آئینہ سازم
من آنم کہ از زہر نوشینہ سازم

(پیامِ مشرق، ص ۱۱۴)

A Dialogue between God and Man

GOD

I created the world with the same water and clay
But you created Iran, Turkey and Ethiopia.
From the earth I brought forth pure iron,
But you made from it sword, arrow and gun.
You made an axe from the garden tree
And a cage for the singing bird.

MAN

You created the night, I created a lamp,
You created the clay, I fashioned a cup,
You created deserts, hills and mountain slopes,
I created meadows, orchards and gardens.
I am the one to make mirror out of stone,
I am the one to prepare sweet wine out of poison[9]

Such bold and enlightened expressions of self-realization were used extensively by Iqbal in his poetry and philosophy. Thus, in Iqbal's view, humanity has limitless potential and qualities and with this creativity is capable of accomplishing the tasks for which they were created.

In some other poems Iqbal presents a very heartfelt longing and desire to cling to his Creator which shows his intense love of God as well as his intimacy with Him. Here he implores God to reveal Himself and embrace him with passion.

Love is in veil and so is Beauty
Either you reveal Yourself or make me manifest.
You are a boundless ocean and I a mere rivulet!
Either You embrace me or discard me!
If I am a seashell in Your hands is the honour of
my pearl,
And if I am broken shell, You make me an imperial
jewel.
On the Day of Judgement when the register of my
deeds is presented
You would feel embarrassed and so would I.[10]

In *Javed Nāmah* travelling through the seven heavens Zindah Rūd (a pseudonym Iqbal adopted for himself) finally approaches the Beauty, an Aspect of God. Here the poem deals with the everlasting quest of the soul, the human struggle against sin and the search for salvation, peace and glory. In the final part of the poem Zindah Rūd asks:

Who am I? Who art Thou? Where is the world?
Why is there a distance between me and Thee?
Say, why am I in the bonds of destiny?
Why dost Thou die not, whilst I die?[11]

The Voice of Beauty replies:

You have been in the world of dimensionate,
And any contained therein, therein dies,
If you seek life, advance your *khūdī*,
Drown the world's dimensions in yourself.

You shall then behold who I am and who you are
How you died in the world, how you lived.[12]

Zauq wa Shauq is a very moving poem, full of natural imagery, and is one of the masterpieces of Iqbal's poems in *Bāl-i-Jibra'īl*. Towards the end of the poem the last stanza states the conflicting attitudes held by the poet:

At the very moment of my encounter I have
no courage to look
Although my impudent gaze keeps seeking
some excuses.[13]

Thus, in Iqbal's poetry there is a very subtle and conflicting struggle; at times he approaches God with boldness and impertinence, yet has very deep love and respect for Him as well.

3

The Universe

Open your eyes and see the earth,
The sky, the space and the rising sun.[14]

According to the Qur'ānic teachings this vast universe is not created without design and purpose. Modern scientific thought is that this world and the entire universe is an accidental occurrence. However, those who truly reflect on the creation of the universe humbly proclaim: "O our Lord! You have not created this without any purpose". (3:191)

Iqbal in his poetry constantly portrays the natural beauty of the universe and he is fascinated by rivers, mountains, clouds, stars and the moon as well as flowers, birds and animals.

This universe is not static and, as science has discovered, it is expanding all the time. There are changes, mutations and transformations happening regularly. Thus the universe is forever evolving and continues its journey towards its completion. Iqbal alluded to this fact as:

> The universe still looks incomplete.
> A voice forever repeats *Be and it becomes*.[15]

Be and it becomes is the Qur'ānic expression *kun fayakun* (36: 82). This refers to the act of creation when God says: "*Kun*–Be" and it instantly happens. His command is instantaneously obeyed and whatever He orders comes into being. For Iqbal this universe is still an unfinished entity constantly undergoing change and development. Thus, it provides a stimulus to humanity's creative activity to achieve perfection by the power of their *khūdī* (self).

The Qur'ān stresses that human beings should reflect on the signs which are scattered all around them and should subdue and control the forces of nature as he is the vicegerent of God on Earth and as such have a role to play in shaping the universe. In this way humanity is required to display its creative faculty and unless its takes this initiative he will not be fulfilling his role in this world. Iqbal alludes to this in his poem *Insān (Man)*:

> If he wills he can change the shape of the garden;
> This creature is wise, full of insight and strong.[16]

The other aspect of the universe is its beauty which evokes appreciation and our sense of aesthetics. Iqbal wrote a number of poems celebrating the beauty of nature. He has skillfully depicted the beautiful and exotic scenery in his poem *Zauq wa Shauq* – (*Ecstasy*) which he wrote in Palestine.

> Life of passion and delight–breaking of dawn in the desert:
> Radiant brooks flowing from the spring of sunrise.
> Eternal Beauty tearing the veil, revealing itself:
> Dazzling the eyes but enriching the soul.
> Multi-coloured night clouds left hazy mist
> Clothing the Mount Iṣnam[17] in beautiful attire.
> Air is pure and pleasant; date-palm leaves washed clean:
> The sand around Kāzimah[18] feels soft like velvet sheen.[19]

Another masterpiece of literary composition–*Saqī Nāmah* (*To the Cup-bearer*) portrays the arrival of spring. Here is the opening passage:

> The caravan of spring has pitched
> Its tents; these hillsides are bewitched—
> Lily, narcissus and rose have come,
> And the poppy from age-old martyrdom
> Red-shrouded, with colours to hide earth's face;
> Through rock itself hot pulses race;
> Blue, blue the skies, with calm winds blest,

No winged thing loiters in its nest.
Down from the heights that rill comes leaping,
Slipping, spurting, recoiling, creeping,
Stumbling, recovering, while it winds
Through a hundred turnings until it finds
Its way, gnawing through boulders that block
Its channel, through mountain—hearts of rock!
Oh *Sāqī* fair as the poppy, see
How it sings life's message! Pour for me
–Rose–harvest is not every day!—
A fiery wine to purge away
All veils, wine to paint life's soul bright:
That wine, the uttermost worlds' delight,
That holds the eternal rapture, betrays
The eternal secret:—oh *Sāqī*, raise![20]

Here Iqbal displays with great accuracy the details of the arrival of spring. At times it is very emotional and sensuous but this displays his acute observation and powerful imagination captivating the hearts of readers.

According to Iqbal, observation of the universe and reflecting upon it, is essential for acquiring *ma'rifah* (knowledge) of God. As the universe is the external manifestation of God. This universe displays innumerable qualities of God: command, creation, guidance, mercy, provision, control and supremacy just to name a few. We cannot see God, but we see His gracious qualities which give us an indication of His Presence. As Iqbal has said:

Witness of His glory in this assembly of existence;
Dependency is evident in the entire universe.[21]

4

Time and Space

There is neither time nor space;
Nothing exists absolutely except God.[22]

*T*ime and space are some important yet controversial
age-old topics that Iqbal has also dealt with in his
writings. Iqbal deeply believed in the spiritual basis
of the universe, he did not attribute a materialistic
interpretation to time and space. For him both time
and space are the creative actions of God through
which He expresses His complete supremacy and
penetrative wisdom. The quintessence of the universe
is its unity, yet as human beings observe its external
manifestation, it appears to them as multiplicity. To
the human intellect, the universe seems to be static
yet in fact it is in constant motion throughout its
journey in time and space. Thus Iqbal pertinently
states:

Every atom throbs with life;
Rest is an illusion;
Life's journey pauses not
For every moment is new glory.[23]

Inertia is impossible in the universe;
Nothing is constant but change.[24]

Iqbal is appreciative of Albert Einstein's (1879–1955) Theory of Relativity as it demolished the ancient concept of materialism. However, he criticized his theory for considering time as the fourth dimension, the length, breadth and depth being the other three. Iqbal maintained if time is to be the fourth dimension then just as the past is considered determined and fatalistic, the future will be considered the same. Thus he observed that if time is to be considered the fourth dimension then it loses the importance of its creative action.

According to Iqbal, God's creative activity may appear outwardly as a process of change in serial time. In reality, this change is the unceasing act of God in durational time. God wants to test humanity's creative ability, hence if creative acts are performed by a dynamic and strong personality they live as permanent forces across serial time. Otherwise, all human acts are doomed to perish. According to Iqbal this concept is nothing less than "permanence in change". He explained this concept beautifully in his poem *Masjid-i-Qurṭubah* (*The Mosque of Cordova*). He wrote this whilst visiting the mosque and reflecting upon the lost splendour of Islamic Spain. Here one finds Iqbal's exposition of his concept of time and the world's transitory nature. The opening lines are as follows:

> The succession of day and night is the contriver of events.
> The succession of day and night is the essence of life and death.
> The succession of day and night is two-tone silken threads,
> That weaves the cloak displaying Divine attributes.[25]

And the concluding couplet of this stanza is:

> The beginning and the end, hidden or manifest – all annihilation;
> Be it old or new, the final destination of all is annihilation.[26]

This is Iqbal's description of the destructive power of serial time which perishes all human efforts. However, in the latter part of the poem, Iqbal maintains that if man is inspired by the courageous power of love and dedication, this cannot be destroyed by time. Iqbal's visit to the Mosque and its magnificent architecture inspired him to foresee that if Muslims realized their ego both individually and collectively they would attain the heights of perfection again. He believed that the Muslim world was ready for such a revolution which would change its destiny.

Towards the end of *Bāng-i-Darā* we come across his poem *Khiḍr-i-Rāh* (*The Guide*). Here Iqbal's concept of time is of ceaseless duration. For him life cannot be measured in serial time as it is ever flowing:

> Measure it not by the scale of day today,
> Eternal, overflowing and evergreen is life.[27]

As regards his philosophy of space Iqbal believes that God is the First and the Last. We with our limited knowledge are unable to comprehend His mysteries. Hence space–time is only an intellectual frame for us to comprehend God's creative activity. As such, he expressed this concept in many verses:

> God is the essence of space and spacelessness,
> Space is nothing but a mode of His expression.[28]

In one of his lectures on *The Reconstruction of Religious Thought in Islam* Iqbal stated:

> Nature is not static fact situated in an a-dynamic void, but a structure of events possessing the character of a continuous creative flow which thought cuts up into isolated immobilities out of whose mutual relations arise the concepts of space and time.[29]

Thus, according to Iqbal, space, time and matter express the free creative energy of God. They are not independent realities existing per se, but only intellectual modes of apprehending the life of God.[30]

> Reality is eternal and spaceless
> Say not that the universe is limitless
> It is empty within from top to bottom
> Yet it is expanding from without.

5

Life

∽∽∽

برتر از اندیشۂ سُود و زیاں ہے زندگی
ہے کبھی جاں اور کبھی تسلیمِ جاں ہے زندگی

تُو اسے پیمانۂ امروز و فردا سے نہ ناپ
جاودداں، پیہم دواں ، ہر دم جواں ہے زندگی

اپنی دُنیا آپ پیدا کر اگر زِندوں میں ہے
سرّ آدم ہے ، ضمیرِ کُن فکاں ہے زندگی

زندگانی کی حقیقت کوہکن کے دل سے پُوچھ
جُوئے شیر و تیشہ و سنگِ گراں ہے زندگی

بندگی میں گھٹ کے رہ جاتی ہے اِک جُوئے کم آب
اور آزادی میں بحرِ بے کراں ہے زندگی

آشکارا ہے یہ اپنی قوتِ تسخیر سے
گرچہ اِک مٹی کے پیکر میں نہاں ہے زندگی

قلزمِ ہستی سے تو اُبھرا ہے مانندِ حباب
اس زیاں خانے میں تیرا امتحاں ہے زندگی

خام ہے جب تک تو ہے مٹی کا اِک انبار تو
پُختہ ہو جائے تو ہے شمشیرِ بے زنہار تو

(بانگِ درا، ص ۲۷۲،۲۷۱)

Life is above the fear of profit and loss,
At times worth preserving, whilst surrendering
it sometimes.
Measure it not with today and tomorrow.
Life is everlasting, constantly moving
and evergreen.
Set up your own world, if you are alive!
Discern you then the secret of creation
"Be and it becomes."[31]
Learn the reality of life from a mountain digger
Life is struggle with a pickaxe to dig a stream of milk.[32]
In submission life's stream is constrained
into a trickle
While liberty makes it a boundless ocean!
Life is aware of its power of triumph
Yet concealed in the handful of dust!
You emerged from the ocean of existence like a bubble
Now is your test in this hostile battle.

If you are raw, you are only a heap of dust,
Attaining maturity turns you into a merciless sword![33]

*K*hiḍr-i-Rāh is one of the very long poems in *Bāng-i-Dara* in which Iqbal has discussed several social, economic and political problems facing the world in general with particular reference to the affairs of the Muslim *ummah*. For this he chose Khiḍr (who guided the Prophet Mūsā (peace be upon him) on a journey) as his guide. In this imaginary conversation one of the questions Iqbal raised with him was about the secret of life. Part of the reply of Khiḍr is quoted above which expounds Iqbal's philosophy of life.

Life is precious, yet it is above valuation and although its preservation is vital, one should be ready to sacrifice it for a noble cause. One should not rely on the efforts of others but be ready to struggle and create one's own world. This will require untold efforts as illustrated by the diligent efforts of Farhād carving out the canal in a mountain. Life needs boundless freedom to express its exuberance otherwise it could not express its potentialities. This in fact was a wake-up call for the Muslim *ummah* that if it did not rise up it would be worthless in the world. It had to get ready and acquire maturity to regain its lost prestige.

Iqbal believed in the spiritual basis of the universe and life. This is not just his religious belief but he came to this conclusion by his deep study and reflection on scientific and philosophical views and opinions. Undoubtedly, he did not deny the external manifestation of time and space but he did not consider them to be the only realities. Thus, he believed that although human beings have to live in this world, their essence is not of this world.

> The fire that is in you has not come
> Out of this heap of dust.
> You have not come out of this world
> This world is there because of you.[34]

Ultimately, humanity is destined to reach the higher plane and they should strive for this goal as Iqbal said:

> In the wilderness of my insanity Jibra'īl is a
> small prey
> O Valiant Soul! Get hold of the Divine Being.[35]

Iqbal in one of his poems – *Falsafa–i–Gham*–gave a profound exposition of the philosophy of grief. He realized that human beings are a unique form of creation. Their life is a curious combination of joys and sorrows. Thus, they have to live in this world and experience both happiness and difficulties. They have to learn to live with them. A person always forgets the pleasures of life, but sorrows and afflictions always haunt them. However, the grief and sorrow, failures and sufferings ultimately have a sobering influence on human beings. These experiences help refine their character and ultimately make them a better human being.

> The wine of life is embodiment of pleasure,
> Yet it carries grief like a cloud trickling tears.
> The bubble of life dances on the waves of grief;
> Grief is a vital chapter of the book of life.[36]

Thus, setbacks stimulate a person to renew their efforts and failures spur them on to make more effort. Progress towards perfection requires constantly jumping hurdles to achieve success.

According to Iqbal, death is not the end of life, although there is a temporary separation between the body and soul. Death overtakes the physical body and the human Ego remains immortal.

> We part in this lower world to meet again,
> We deem these temporary partings as permanent and lament.
> People die, yet they do not annihilate
> Really they don't get separated from us.[37]

6

Death and Immortality of Soul

Ah! This world, a place to grieve for the young
and old!
Imprisoned in the magic of today and tomorrow!
How difficult is life! How easy to die!
Worthless like wind, death is cheap!
Quakes and thunderbolts, famines and afflictions,
How varied are Time's ticks and tribulations.
Death prevails in a poor man's hut, in a rich
man's villa.
Death is ever-present in cities and wilderness.
Death is tumultuous in a silent sea
Yet boats get drowned in the lap of waves.
Lips are sealed. None can complain.
Life like a yoke–throat choking constrain.[38]

The imprudent assumes death as the end of life;
This evening of life heralds the morn of
perennial life.[39]

*E*legy is a serious meditative poem by a reflective mind lamenting everything that is lost and gone or absent. It is a poetic form of paying tribute to the departed soul. Thus, sorrow and love became the principal themes of the elegy. Iqbal has followed this tradition and written many elegies for notable Urdu poets and other personalities. The one most memorable and touching is in the memory of his mother, part of which is quoted above.

In this long poem Iqbal contemplates the inevitability of death and that everything in the universe is subject to decay and death. Thus, one learns to live with this reality. One can mourn, but consolation lies in the knowledge that nothing could have been done. For Iqbal, it is only a temporary absence, a curtain of sleep which will end. Death does not perish the soul.

Life is a constant theme in Iqbal's poetry. It emerges as a positive concept, which is vibrant and warm. It is everlasting, constantly moving and evergreen. It is not just breathing in and out and it is not to be measured with today and tomorrow. Above all, life is beyond the fear of profit and loss. His belief was that, despite being made of clay, man was destined for life after death, and his soul would live on. Death is only a temporary break and without death there could not be any concept of life.

In the physical world we see the struggle to preserve the continuity of progeny. Flowers bloom and then die but they produce enough seeds to continue the process of the preservation of their species. Thus, individuals die yet the act of procreation continues. A human being, however, is on a different level of existence. As God has breathed soul into them, so they like God are immortal. Iqbal compares death to sleep, and thereby humanity progresses to the eternal world. By death the body of a person steps into a new life. Yet according to Iqbal, real death is life without conviction and life without a goal.

> In the world beyond
> Life stalked for death,
> But the impulse to procreate
> Peopled the world of man and beast.
> Flowers blossomed and dropped
> From this tree of life.
> Fools think life is ephemeral;
> Life renews itself forever–
> Moving fast as a flash,
> Moving to eternity in a breath!
> Time, a chain of days and nights,
> Is the ebb and flow of breath.[40]

Iqbal urges one to remain constantly alert and capture death as if it is a prey so that one's own evolution does not stop. According to him, a person's real enemy is their death. Whenever they encounters it the struggle is fierce yet they should try to defeat it:

O Eternal Being! You fear death
Death is your prey and you have to lie in
ambush.[41]

In another poem he describes man as a lion and
death like a deer, the former ever ready to pounce
upon the latter. Death in the guise of sleep gives a
message of life:

Death is the name of a taste for revival of life.
It gives a message of life through the curtain
of sleep.
The essence of man does not know non-
existence,
He disappears from sight yet does not annihilate.[42]

No doubt Iqbal believed in the immortality of the
soul and eternal life, as he expressed quite often:

If our death would be a permanent death,
God would be ashamed of His deed.[43]

7

God and the Devil

Both God and the Devil give man opportunities only,
leaving him to make use in the way he thinks fit.

"Think of the Devil and he is sure to appear".
This is equally true of God.
Stray Thoughts. Pp.121–2.

*I*qbal in his many poems has discussed the role played by Satan (the Devil), which in Arabic is *Shaytān*, while Iblīs is his proper name used in the Qur'ān. He was the one who tempted the Prophet Adam (peace be upon him) and his wife and was responsible for their expulsion from *Jannah*. Satan and his offspring were given reprieve till the Day of Judgement to misguide the progeny of Adam. Thus, there is an eternal conflict between the two species.

Iqbal was fascinated by the strategy of Satan and he has tried to unravel the psychological framework of his personality in an emphatic way. In a long poem entitled *Jibra'īl wa Iblīs*, Iqbal recorded an imaginary conversation between the two. Jibra'īl (Gabriel) re-monstrated Iblīs, that he had lost his exalted position because of his refusal to bow down to Ādam. Iblīs justifies himself with the following:

> With my boldness I make this handful
> of dust rise up.
> My mischief weaves the garment that
> reason wears.
> From the shore you watch the clash of
> good and evil.
> Which of us suffers the buffets of storms –
> you or I?
> Both Khiḍr[44] and Ilyās[45] feel helpless;
> The storms I have stirred up rage in oceans,
> rivers and streams.
> If you are alone with God, ask Him:
> Whose blood coloured the story of Adam?
> I rankle in God's heart like a thorn. But
> what about you?
> All you do is chant: 'He is God' over
> and over.[46]

Iqbal skilfully presenting Satan's point of view ex-pressed that due to him there is so much commotion and activity taking place in the world otherwise there would be deadly silence. Iqbal has presented Satan as being stubborn and trying to justify his previous stand. With all his faults Satan comes out as a bold figure and evokes some sympathy for his predicament. Iqbal has not expressed this view explicitly.

The most interesting poem is the one that records the proceedings of the Advisory Council of Iblīs. Iqbal's imaginative mind produces an eavesdrop transcript of the consultation which Iblīs had with his advisors. They discuss issues raging in the world and how Iblīs and his five companions' manipulations are causing political upheaval and revolutions in human society. How the Muslim world was made to lose its way by indulging in false Sufism which makes a man inactive and passive, and the dissensions caused by the manoeuvring of petty religious leaders and kings. Other advisors referred to the Russian Revolution which brought oppressed people to the top. Iblīs discounts all the apprehensions of his advisors and says: "I am really fearful of the awakening of the *ummah*". Thus, in order to keep check on its revival he advises his deputies to keep them busy in trivial affairs:

> Keep them intoxicated in the chanting and rhythmic recitation
> Make them firm in the monastic way of life.[47]

In a more direct poem entitled *Iblīs's Command to his Political Heirs*, Iqbal has recorded the practical steps which Iblīs is ordering to bring about the downfall of the *ummah*.

The poor who are not afraid of death
Remove the soul of Muḥammad from their body.
Give the Arabs Western ideologies,
Banish Islam from Ḥijāz and Yemen.
The remedy of Afghans' sense of honour is
Remove the religious leaders from their abode.[48]

The lesson which Iqbal wants to convey is that this *ummah* should remain on its guard against the tricks and temptations of Satan.

8

Clash of Good and Evil

From Eternity till now there remains a
constant struggle
Between the lamp of the Chosen One[49] and
the flame of Abū Lahab.[50]

Belief in good and evil are part of the Islamic faith. It
is God Who "imbued it [soul] with (the conscious-
ness of) its evil and piety." (al-Shams 91: 8) It means
that the Creator has imbedded in a person's nature
tendencies and inclinations towards both good and
evil. Although it is God who created these tendencies
of good and evil, He also endowed humanity with
volition. A person is free to choose the path of piety
or evil. They are not like minerals, plants or animals
that are bound by laws of nature and which they have
to follow. Humanity, that is the best of creation, was
given the faculty to think and ponder in choosing

their course of action. They could foresee the con-
sequences of their actions. Thus, God has declared:
"Surely We showed him the Right Path, regardless
of whether he chooses to be thankful or ungrateful
(to his Lord)." (al-Dahr 76: 3) This is what Iqbal
referred to when he said that pleasantness or misery
depends on one's own actions.

> Actions shape life into Heaven or Hell.
> Man in his nature is neither destined to Paradise
> nor to Hell.[51]

According to Iqbal, volition given to a person to
choose the path of righteousness or disobedience is
vital because if a person is constrained and he has no
freedom of action then there is no value in goodness.

In this discussion the role played by Satan
(or Iblīs – a name used in the Qur'ān) is crucial.
His rebellion and disobedience of God led to his
downfall. However, he sought respite until the Day
of Judgement so that he can instigate Adam and
his progeny to disobey God's commandments. God
granted him this opportunity. Hence this eternal
conflict has continued ever since. In *Jannah*, where
Adam with his spouse were staying, Satan tempted
them by saying that your Lord has forbidden you
to approach this tree only to prevent you from
becoming angels or immortals. Satan's temptation
landed them in this world. Satan has ever since set

off this struggle between good and evil. Iqbal in his two poems: *Jibra'īl wa Iblīs* and *Nāla'-i-Iblīs* gives penetrating insight into Satan's psychological explanation of his actions in an empathic way. Thus, he complains to God:

> Lord of good and evil!
> Adam's company has corrupted me.
> He never questioned my commands;
> Shutting his eyes and he failed to discover himself.

Then he contemptuously says:

> What is this man? A handful of straw;
> Only a spark from me is sufficient for this straw.[52]

In this way he justified his disobedience pointing out the frailty and inferiority of Adam and his progeny.

Iqbal was influenced by Western thinkers and while studying in Germany his admiration for Goethe's *Faust* was born. This was Goethe's *magnum opus* and the greatest work of German literature. In it, Goethe describes the relationship of God and man, good and evil and the whole meaning of life. Iqbal has tried to reconcile the goodness and omnipotence of God with the immense volume of evil in His creation. Agreeing with Goethe that evil is obverse of good, he asserts that both form a higher unity. Though there are errors, imperfections and conflicts occurring in human life, despite these shortcomings, basically human life is innately good. This is what Iqbal has to say in *Payām-i-Mashriq*:

> How should I describe good and evil?
> The problem is so complex that the tongue falters.
> Outside the bough you see flowers and thorns,
> Inside it there is neither flower nor thorn![53]

Iqbal emphasizes that there is no life without evil. Unless there is constant struggle against evil, life is not worth living. If life is smooth it becomes boring.

9

Predestination

Dependent on predestination has become
their mode of action
In whose determination was hidden God's destiny.[54]

Destiny (*Taqdīr*) is one the most controversial philosophical and ethical topics which has been debated for centuries. In every age scholars, philosophers, theologians and Sufis indulged in the controversy of whether humanity is free in whatever it wants to do or bound by its destiny. The problem of free will and coercion has yet to be solved. A group of Muslim thinkers believe that a person is responsible for their actions as God has given them freedom of action and they are free to choose whatever they want to do. Whereas another group of thinkers and Sufis maintain that humanity is really helpless and whatever has been destined for them from eternity will happen.

In fact both these groups of scholars are taking extreme positions in advancing their view points, which is not helpful in resolving the issue. If one were to consider this problem dispassionately then one finds that humanity is constrained as well as independent. They are neither fully independent nor entirely constrained in the task that they want to perform. Thus, a person's life is composed of both compulsion and free will.

According to Iqbal nothing is absolutely predestined. There is an important element of novelty and evolution. The whole universe is still evolving and progressing towards its goal of completion. If we do not accept this then we have to believe that after the creation of the universe God is not performing any creative activity. This Iqbalian concept is based on the Qur'an: "A new mighty task engages Him each day." (al-Raḥmān 55: 29) Thus Iqbal compares life to a 'flowing river' and 'young wine'.

> Life is a flowing river and it should flow
> This old wine is still young and it should
> remain young.[55]

In *Javid Nāmah* where Iqbal begins his journey through the universe he narrates his meeting with Zarvan, an angel of Time and Space who accompanies him in these celestial wanderings. Zarvan acquaints Iqbal with the mysteries of life and destiny and that every happening is controlled by His order. This echoes the Qur'ānic verse that even a leaf does not fall without the knowledge of God (al-An'ām 6: 59). Nevertheless, Iqbal believes that humanity has the capacity to shape the destiny of the universe around them and in this process of gradual change they are accompanied by God. A person has a capacity to bring about changes in their life by education and training. They can acquire new skills and mould their life. Although they could never be fully independent but their creative skills give them limited power of action and they are not absolutely helpless nor absolutely free. As such it gives them superiority over other creations. Iqbal has tried to express this tricky problem of compulsion and freewill thus:

> I am not free and nor can I say that I am
> constrained,
> I am a living earthling in the midst of
> revolution.

Iqbal was of the opinion that history is not predetermined events which unfold slowly before us but rather it is ever-changing events which evolved before us. He has beautifully depicted the ever changing events in his poem *Time*.

> What was, has faded: what is, is fading: but
> these words few can tell their worth;
> Time still gapping with expectation of what is
> nearest its hour of birth.

New tidings slowly come drop by drop from my
pitcher gurgling of time's new sights,
As I count over the beads strung out on my
threaded rosary of days and nights.[56]

Iqbal accepts that predestination has a place in God's
scheme of things. There are laws of nature which
govern the lives of animals and birds. It is also ap-
plicable to plants and vegetation as well as minerals.
Similarly the sun and the moon, the planets and stars
are regulated by Divine decree and they have no free
will. In one of his poems *Divine Commandments*,
Iqbal has tried to shed light on the two different
aspects of *Taqdīr* (Destiny):

Following the Destiny or following Orders?
This is not a difficult problem, O wise man!
Instantly the Destiny changes hundreds of time,
Its follower is sad at times and happy at others.
Fettered by predestination are vegetation and stones
A Muslim is bound only by Divine orders.[57]

Destiny is not something written in a stone that does
not change; hence one should obey God's command-
ments and leave one's destiny under Divine orders.
There is a hadith which says *Du'ā* to Allah may
change destiny if He feels that it will help the man.

10

Reason and Love

Daringly love jumped in Nimrūd's fire.
While intellect is absorbed in the spectacle
from a roof-top.[58]

*H*ere Iqbal graphically contrasts the difference between the attitude of passionate love and reasoning. Nimrūd was the king at the time of the Prophet Ibrāhīm (peace be upon him) who had a fire prepared into which he threw young Ibrahim. The Prophet, immersed in deep love of God, did not hesitate to descend into the fire whereas an intellect would have debated the consequences.

One of the major themes in Iqbal's poetry is *'aql* (reason, intellect) and *'ishaq* (love) and the relationship between the two. For each of these words he has used many synonyms. For *'aql* the other words used are *'ilm* (knowledge*),* *khirad* (reason) and philosophy.

He also referred to it as *nūr* (light) and *chirāg-i-rah* (lamp for the path).

> Pass by the reason as this light
> Is the torch for the way and not the destination.[59]

'Ishq acquired a new and comprehensive connotation in Iqbal's poetry. Although in his earlier poetry he used the word following the classical tradition, later on he developed a different meaning and gave it a wider range of connotations making it a powerful force. He also used such synonyms as *junūn* (craze), *shuaq* (ecstasy) and *jazb-i-durūn* (deep and selfless devotion).

Iqbal gives superiority to love over intellect as in human life love plays a vital role. In his poem *'Ilm wa 'Ishq* (*Knowledge and Love*) he vividly contrasted the differences between them. While knowledge is essential, its sphere is limited to sensory perceptions. It is through love that one can penetrate to the heart of the matter.

> Knowledge told me that love is madness.
> Love told me knowledge is conjecture and
> presumption.
> So, O presumptuous one! Don't become a
> bookworm.
> Love is all manifest while knowledge is
> all fuzzy.

Warmth of love raises the struggle in
the universe.
Knowledge identifies attributes; love
reaches the soul.
Love is tranquility and stability. Love
is life and death.
Knowledge poses questions and love
is the hidden answer.

Love is all conviction and conviction
is always victorious.
Knowledge is dependent on books while
love is the source of all books.[60]

However, it does not mean that Iqbal is against
reason. He believes that all human actions and
motivations emanate from love and intellect only
guides them to the right direction. If that ideal whose
love leads to motivation is sound then the intellect
will lead it to the right direction. He was appreciative
of the eminent German philosopher Emmanuel Kant
(1724–1804) who published an influential book
The Critique of Pure Reason in 1718. In this book
Kant attempted to distinguish between the reality
of matter and its appearance. The main thesis of
his philosophical thought was that the knowledge
acquired through perceivable things is not certain.
Real knowledge is above human perception. This
demolished the 18th century rationalist movement.
Yet he failed to reach the real source of knowledge –
the revelation.

Notwithstanding the differences between love and reason which many poems of Iqbal elucidate, both are essential for leading man to a balanced life. It is through reason that man can solve the problems faced in this world and harness the resources to create a better environment. It is through intuition and inspiration that man achieves the breakthrough in all fields of knowledge. Intellect and knowledge can lead man nearer to his destination but without love he could not reach the final goal.

Though reason to the portal guide,
Yet entry to it is denied,
Beg God to grant a lighted heart,
For light and sight are things apart.
Though knowledge lends to mind a glow,
No *houris* its Eden can ever show.
Some passions leave the mind intact,
While others make it blind to fact.[61]

Usually it is the intellect which acts as a guide, yet it is love which is more knowledgeable.

The world thinks that the reason is the torch for the way
Who knows that lunacy also possesses sagacity.[62]

 11

The Qur'ān

Since the advent of the Qur'ān in the world
The signs of soothsayer and the priest got lost.
I proclaim my heart's secret:
This is no mere Book but is quite a different genre.
When it enters the soul, the soul changes
And when the soul changes the whole world change.[63]

This living Book is the Qur'ān, full of wisdom.
Its sagacity is ancient and everlasting.
Its words are without doubt and alteration.
Its verses do not depend on interpretation and change.
It is the last praiseworthy message for mankind,
Carried by the Mercy of the entire Universe.
If you want to live as a Muslim
Then it is impossible to live without the Qur'ān.[64]

For Iqbal the Qur'ān was a unique book. It was not just a book but *al-Kitāb* –The Book, which echoed the Divine melody enriching the mind and the soul.

Its wisdom, beauty, charm and harmony captivated hearts as well as intellects. Iqbal deeply absorbed the Qur'ān in his soul and it captured both his conscious and sub-conscious mind. Hence his writings refer to the Qur'ān, Sunnah as well as Islamic history.

Love of the Qur'ān was inculcated in him from an early age. He used to recite it every day after the dawn prayers. His father advised him to recite the Qur'ān as if it had been revealed upon him directly from God. The reasoning being that if he were to do this, it would penetrate his veins and he would truly understand it. This remark made a lasting impression on him and helped him to imbibe the Holy Book in his emotions and intellect. Later on, expressing this advice to others he wrote this beautiful verse:

> Until the Qur'ān is revealed onto your heart
> Neither Rāzī nor the *Kashshāf's* author can
> unravel its secrets.[65]

Imam Fakhr al-Dīn al-Rāzī (1150–1210) and Imam Abū al-Qāsim al-Zamakhsharī (1075–1144) were two eminent Qur'ānic commentators. *Al-Kashshāf 'An Ḥaqa'iq al-Tanzīl* being the title of the latter's commentary. The author was a rationalist who used to rationalize issues. Imam Razi's *tafsīr Mafatīḥ al-Ghayb* also occasionally discusses in his exegesis giving prominence to reason.

Iqbal believed that after absorbing the Qur'ān, *īmān* (faith) and creed (*'aqīdah*) influenced action (*'aml*).

> Even if the intellect affirmed *Lā Ilah* so what?
> Unless the heart and the insight is not Muslim,
> it is of no use.[66]

According to Iqbal the other important precept is reflection on the universe all around us. The creation of heaven and earth, alteration of day and night and variation of seasons all indicate that there is a purpose behind their creation and it is not just for fun and play. It is the duty of hummankind to reflect on these marvelous happenings all around them. Having reflected, one can harness the forces of nature for the benefit of humanity. One should also reflect on one's own creation. How from a drop of sperm which mingled with the female egg a human being is created, one that grows up and has all the faculties of sight, hearing and reason. Thus, one of the Qur'ān's distinguishing features is its emphasis on the observation of the external world. This led Muslims to deeply reflect on the universe and led them to become leaders of the experimental method of induction. In this way they were truly pioneers of modern science. This Qur'ānic wisdom helped them to develop sciences such as botany, zoology, medicine, mathematics and other sciences at a time when Europe was submerged in the Dark Ages.

Iqbal's poetry certainly revolves around the Qur'ān. One finds innumerable references and citations of Qur'ānic phrases even verses quoted *ad verbatim*. This influence of the Qur'ān runs deep in Iqbal's poetry and is reflected in the dynamic message he so ardently tried to convey to the Muslim *ummah*. The influence of the Qur'ān has produced sublimity and refinement in Iqbal's poetry. As his yearning soul yields such sublime and eloquent discourses they transcend the heart and mind of the recipients.

12

The Prophet
(peace be upon him)

It is he, the essence of wisdom, the last of
the prophets, master of all
Who graced the path's dust with the glory
of the valley of Sinai.
In the eyes of love and ecstasy He is the First
and He is the Last
He is the Qur'ān, He is the Furqān, He is YāSīn
and He is ṬāHā.[67]

ove of the Prophet (peace be upon him) is part of
the faith of every Muslim. There is a tradition which
started during the life of the Prophet (peace be upon
him) of composing *na'at* (eulogy) in his honour and
this practice continued down the centuries in all
languages used by Muslims. Although Iqbal has not
composed *na'at* in the traditional way, his poetry

is the embodiment of the Prophet's (peace be upon him) love.

The verses quoted above are the concluding part of a long poem written as a tribute to Ḥakīm Sanā'ī Ghaznavī (1080–1131) while visiting his tomb in Kabul. Sanai's poetry had a tremendous influence upon Persian literature. He is considered the first poet to use the *qasidah* (ode), *ghazal* (lyric), and the *masnavi* (rhymed couplet) to express the philosophical, mystical and ethical ideas of Sufism. There are numerous references to Qur'ānic expressions in the last two lines: *al-Awwal* (The First) and *al-Akhīr* (The Last) are from Sūrah al-Ḥadīd 57:3 being two attributes of God, al-Furqān (the Criterion) is one of the names of the Qur'ān while YāSīn and ṬāHā are names of two surahs of the Qur'ān. These verses demonstrate Iqbal's deep love for the Prophet (peace be upon him).

In the 20th century Western civilization was dominating the world especially in India which was in the grip of British sovereignty replacing centuries of Muslim rule. In this materialistic atmosphere when Western rationalism was dazzling the sight of everyone and the light of faith and certainty was extinguished, Iqbal sought refuge in the Prophet's love as a tool for survival.

> O the Lord of Yathrib! Help provide me
> the cure
> My reason is afflicted with the West and my
> faith with idolatry.[68]

Wisdom of the West could not dazzle me
I have the antimony from the dust of
Madina and Najaf.[69]

Madina and Najaf being the burial places of the
Prophet (peace be upon him) and 'Ali ibn Abī Ṭalib,
who was the Prophet's nephew (and later son-in-law
being the husband of his daughter Fāṭimah).

Iqbal's longing to perform Hajj and visit Madina
in later life grew very intense. He started composing
Armaghān-i-Ḥijāz (Gift of Ḥijāz) both in Persian and
Urdu, which eventually published posthumously.
However, his deteriorating health did not allow him
to undertake this journey. Whenever the name of the
Prophet (peace be upon him) was mentioned he used
to become agitated due to intense longing and ecstasy.
He used to become tearful. He was also apprehensive
of how, as a person with so many shortcomings and
faults, he could face the Prophet (peace be upon him).
He composed this quatrain imploring God:

(O God!) You are in no need from anyone
and I am a beggar.
On the Day of Judgement please excuse me
from questioning about my deeds.
Of course You will see my account of life,
But please hide it from the sight of the Prophet
(so as not disgrace me in his sight).[70]

For Iqbal the Prophet (peace be upon him) was the
Messenger who brought the final guidance from God

and gave a practical demonstration by implementing the Divine code of life (Shariʻah). Furthermore, he was the one who inspired his Companions as well as Muslims all over the world. Unless Muslims emulate his teachings they could not attain success in this life or the Hereafter. Iqbal put this succinctly in *Jawāb-i-Shikwah* (Response to the Complaint) the reply from God:

> If you remain faithful to Muḥammad
> Then I shall always be with you;
> Leave alone this inconsequential Universe,
> The Tablet, and the Pen, shall be your prize.[71]

The Tablet refers to the figurative slate on which the fate of everyone is written by God. The Pen refers to the figurative stylus used by God to write the fate of every creature. Here God promises if Muslims remain faithful to His Prophet (peace be upon him) they will be the master of their Destiny.

Although Iqbal's earnest desire to visit Madina was not fulfilled, his prayer recorded in *Rumūz-i-Bikhudi* years earlier was partially fulfilled:

> Give my star of fate an enlightened faith.
> Give me burial place under the shadow
> of your wall.
> So that my restless heart and mercurial
> nature find peace

And I could say to the sky see how
peaceful an end I gained.
You have seen my beginning, now
see my end.[72]

He was buried near the boundary wall of Bādshāhī
Mosque in Lahore which is visited by thousands of
Muslims who pray for his soul.

13

The Perfect Man

The unbeliever loses himself in the universe.
While the universe itself is lost in a *Mu'min*.[73]

Can one determine the power of a *Mu'min*'s hand?
The gaze of a *Mard-i-Mu'min* can alter destiny.[74]

One finds several references in Iqbal's writing about
Mard-i-Kāmil (the perfect man). In Islam humanity
is honoured as the best of creation and they are
conferred the title of vicegerent on earth. Iqbal has
based his concept of the perfect man on the vicegerency
of humanity and like Rūmī he was searching for a
perfect person, who could change the destiny of
the nation as well as of the entire world. For such a
person Iqbal considers such qualities as *khūdī* (self-
realization), *faqr* (contentment), *'qal* (intellect) and
'ishq (intense or passionate love). He rediscovered this
elusive person as none other than the man of faith.

He has given many names to this perfect man such as *Mard-i Mu'min* (man of faith), *Mujāhid* (warrior in defence of Islam), *Mard-i-Yaqīn* (man of conviction), *Qalander* (itinerating carefree person, someone free of worldly demands), *Darwish* (indigent yet contended with what one possesses), *Band'a-i-Ṣaḥrahī* (wandering person) or simply as Muslim and *Mu'min*. It is not the visual image of a Muslim thatevokes any appreciative emotions in Iqbal is defined by their internal quality. The Iqbalian concept of *Mard-i-Mu'min* is based on the Qur'ānic concept of *īmān* which requires unflinching conviction and complete devotion to Allah and His Prophet (peace be upon him) (49: 15). Iqbal, the greatest who has realized his self in relation to God, thus, cultivating His attributes in his personal life.

> Constantly there is an ever-new graciousness
> and grandeur of a *Mu'min*
> In his speech and in his character, reflecting
> Divine criterion.
> Overbearing yet forgiving; unblemished
> and absolute
> These four ingredients compose a Muslim.[75]

The four attributes as mentioned in the Qur'ān are: *Qahharī* (overbearing, firmness against disbelief), *Ghaffarī* (quality of forgiving), *Quddūsī* (purity, holiness and piety) and *Jabarūt* (power and suprem-acy). With such Divine qualities the Perfect Man shapes history; develops human potentialities and helps create a just, caring and sharing society. Such a Perfect Man can change the course of history by harnessing the forces of nature and bring peace and tranquility to the world.

Iqbal very graphically portrays the qualities of a *Mard-i-Mu'min* in the following verses:

> This earthly creature is neighbourly with Jibra'īl
> His station is not Bukhara nor is it Badakhshan.
> No one knows this secret that a *Mu'min*
> Who appears to be reciting is in fact the Qur'ān.
> The purpose of Nature is reflected in its desires
> There is a weighing scale in this world as
> well as in the Hereafter.
> He provides comfort which the tulip bud
> experiences in its bosom
> As well as that hurricane thrilling the hearts
> of oceans
> Eternal Divine melody fills his days and night
> Unique harmony like the rhythm of Sūrah
> al-Raḥmān.[76]

This perfect man for Iqbal is the vicegerent of God on earth like Adam, who was sent as *Khalīfah*.[77] This is the person who has realised in themselves the Divine call to act as vicegerent and who has raised their ego to the highest level. The source of Iqbal's thought originated from the treasure house of the Qur'an and the Prophet's life. There are very many passages both in the Holy Qur'ān and Hadith extolling the virtues of a *Mu'min* – a person of faith. His integrity, courage, honesty, fidelity, patience, steadfastness and virtuous life are presented as a model for humanity. Iqbal had before him the inspiring model of the Prophet (peace be upon him) and the pious lives of his Companions and their Successors as well as the example of devout Muslims throughout the history of this *ummah*. Iqbal modeled his concept of *Mard-i-Mu'min* on their lives. His desire was that present-day Muslims should try to cultivate their lives on the models of the people from earlier centuries of Islam so that they can be victorious in this world as well as attain salvation in the Hereafter.

Some of Iqbal's critics considered him to have copied the Nietzschean Superman as an ideal for Muslims. However, unlike Nietzsche's Superman, who is the torchbearer of atheism, materialism and authoritarianism, Iqbal has presented the character of the Perfect Man with contrasting attributes of faith, compassion and generosity. Nietzsche did not believe in spirituality whereas for Iqbal faith and love of God and His Prophet are the fountainhead of his philosophy. Iqbal deeply studied Western thought and absorbed what was useful and beneficial and with the amalgam of Islamic teachings and culture produced what Mawlana Sulaiman Nadvi (1884–1953) has aptly described as a beautiful combination of the East and the West.

14

Shāhīn (The Eagle)

I have abandoned that world,
Where subsistence is water and food.
I enjoy the solitude of wilderness
From eternity my nature is retiring.
Neither zephyr nor flower-gatherer nor nightingale
Nor the amorous love stricken song.
Beware of the companions
Their coquetry is ravishing
The strike of victorious youth
Devastated by the wind of wilderness
The life of an eagle is ascetic.
It is not hungry for sparrow or a pigeon
To strike and return soaring high and strike again
Is just a way of keeping the blood warm.
This East and West is the world of partridges
Mine is the azure sky, the limitless vacuum.
I am the darwish of the kingdom of birds
As a falcon builds no nest.[78]

*I*n Iqbal's literary composition both in Urdu and Persian *shāhīn* (eagle) occupies a fundamental and central character. He was searching for an appropriate and suitable character which could represent the qualities of a *Mard-i-Darwish* the word he has often used as synonym for *Mard-i-Mu'min*. *Darwish*, *faqīr* and *qalandar* are the other words Iqbal has used to describe the characteristics of a man of faith. It means a person with few needs who remains content with what they possess and is not tempted by the pomp and glitter of worldly assets. One who chooses to live the life of an ascetic. His fertile imagination found the equivalent of *Mard-i-Mu'min* in the form of the *shāhīn* (the white royal falcon). A majestic bird of prey that does not seek its food from the leftovers of others, it soars high and its vision is beyond the limits of the skies. It does not build a proper nest but just rests on hard rock. It never tires of flying and struggling. It is a courageous and powerful bird as well as being fiercely independent. Iqbal used the metaphor of *shāhīn* extensively just as he did that of other species such as the '*Uqāb* (eagle) and *Bāz* (hawk) to compare the life of a *Mu'min*. In contrast he deprecated vultures, crows and sparrows, as they are scavengers, and are weak and timid. Many of his verses charmingly illustrate his views:

> They both fly in the same sphere
> Yet the world of a vulture is quite different from
> that of a falcon.[79]

Shāhīn is the perfect model of a *Mard-i-Mu'min* and Iqbal chose it as an exceptionally elegant way to portray his image.

Dr Javed Iqbal explained the five distinct features of a *shāhīn* in one of his lectures, which are summarized below:[80]

1. A *Shāhīn* possesses exceptionally keen and acute eyesight, hence the idiom *eagle-eyed*. Thus, a *Mu'min* should have the vision to see beyond the superficial and read between events.

2. A *Shāhīn* is the most fearless of all bird species and it flies at high altitudes. It does not gather food like sparrows and crows, but flies and lives on a different and higher level.

3. A *Shāhīn* eats what it hunts itself. Unlike vultures, which are some of the largest birds but scavenge the leftovers of other animals.

> Amorous eyes seek the enlivened heart
> A dead prey is not suitable for an eagle.[81]

4. A *Shāhīn* seeks solitude. It's not a social bird like sparrows and gulls that live in groups. Solitude is a key part of self-discovery.

5. A *Shāhīn* does not make a nest but just rests on a few sticks on rocks. It lives, eats and breeds in mountains.

> Your abode is not on the dome of a
> royal palace

You, a falcon, should live on a
mountainous rock.[82]

It just survives in the wilderness of
mountains
It is a disgrace for a falcon to build
a nest.[83]

Iqbal warns that falcon's chicks should not be in the
company of other inferior birds like the vulture and
crow. This will impede their spirits:

That deceived falcon brought up with vultures
How can it know the customs of falcons.[84]

A crow could not acquire the art of lofty flight
The company of crows spoilt the falcon chick[85]

Addressing the men of faith, Iqbal asks them to em-
ulate the life of a falcon:

If you're bare-headed, cultivate lofty
determination
Only a falcon deserves the royal headgear.[86]

You are a falcon; your life is to fly
Yet, there are still many skies before you.[87]

A falcon never tires of flying and dropping downs
If you have strength be not fearful of falling.[88]

Thus, the qualities which Iqbal wants a *Mard-i-Mu'min* to emulate from the falcon are sharp vision, swift movement, daring spirit and soaring high in the sky. Live a life without collecting possession, like a falcon that does not build a nest.

15

Unity of the Ummah

With mutual attraction the universe is stable
This fact is hidden in the life of stars.[89]

*I*qbal was very much concerned about the slow
dis-integration of the *ummah*. Loss of political
power and the abolition of the *Khilāfah* led to the
creation of many Muslim countries that were still
under colonial rule and were trying to fashion their
own destinies in isolation. He was much grieved
with the utter devastation of the centres of Muslim
civilization in the Ḥijāz, Egypt, Iraq, Syria, Iran,
Turkey and India. In desperation he addresses the
soul of the Prophet (peace be upon him) expressing
his anguish and heartache:

The deceased *ummah* is utterly disorganized
You tell us please where a Muslim should go?[90]

He was passionately urging for the unity of the *ummah* and praying:

> Muslims should be united to safeguard the
> Ka'bah
> Right from the shores of the Nile to the length
> and breadth of Kashghar.[91]

The desire of unity alone did not satisfy him and his sight was constantly searching for the way to achieve this. He was looking for the causes of this precarious situation which was afflicting the *ummah*. His analysis led him to conclude that the West had tried to disintegrate the Muslim *ummah* by implanting the notion of nationalism, thus dividing them under different nations. So he observes:

> Division of nations is the policy of the West.
> The Islam desires the unity of man.[92]

Then he boldly declared that nationalism has become like a god and its worshippers have lost the straight path designated by Allah.

> The nation is the biggest of these new gods
> Its attire is the shroud of religion.[93]

> Humanity is divided in different nations
> Eroding the roots of the nationality of Islam.[94]

Having identified the causes that are disintegrating the *ummah*, Iqbal tried to warn Muslims of the snares laid down by the West to trap them and he constantly urged them to unite under the banner of Islam disregarding their nationalities and colours.

> This is an Indian and that is a Khurasani;
> This is an Afghani, and that is a Torani,
> O you attached to the shore! Jump
> And become boundless ocean.
> Your wings are contaminated
> with colour and race;
> O you bird of Ḥaram! Perish
> Before flying.[95]

> Destroy the idols of colour and blood.
> Once submerge in the *ummah*
> Neither Torani nor Irani
> Nor Afghani remains in existence.[96]

Iqbal maintains that the basis of Islam is not nationality but Declaration of Faith in the Oneness of God and the Messengership of the Prophet (peace be upon him). Even the close relations of the Prophet (peace be upon him) and the inhabitants of his city became *millat* of *kufr* (a clan of infidels) when rejecting the message of Islam whereas Salmān, the Persian and Ṣuhaib of Rūm became part of the Muslim *ummah*. Iqbal urges Muslims not to think that their *millat* is of the same composition as nationalities of the West.

The basis of their community is not nation, language or colour, for Muslims their unity is on the basis of religion. This message is also repeated in his essays and letters. Urging Muslims to return to the lost path of Islam he wrote:

> One lesson which I have learnt from Islamic history is that it is Islam that helped to sustain Muslims in their difficult times and not Muslims. If today you focus your sights on Islam and inspired by its life-giving thoughts, then your scattered and disintegrated forces will roll back and unite.[97]

It is a pity that Muslims have not heeded Iqbal's call for the *ummah's* unity. Sadly it is now further divided by schools of *fiqh*, misinterpretation of the real Sufism and cultural practices that are not sanctioned by Islam.

16

Causes of the Downfall of Muslims

The Muslims are no more on earth, there is a
loud furore
We say, 'Were Muslims here at all? Why is
this false uproar?'
Christian in appearance, by culture Hindu,
though not as yet in name.
Can these be Muslims? Seeing them would
put the Jews to shame.
Sayyids, Mirzas and Afghāns – such titles
as you fit.
You are anything else but Muslim, Be honest
and admit.[98]

The early part of the 20th century was a very gloomy
period for the Muslim *ummah*. After the First World
War (1914–18) most of the territory ruled by the

Ottoman Caliphate was grabbed by the British and
French colonial powers and Muslims in Eastern
Europe were driven out. The Russian Revolution
resulted in the loss of Muslim rule in Central Asia.
Egypt was under British rule and North Africa
under French domination. Muslims in India found
themselves in a minority after the British destroyed
the Moghul Empire. Iqbal's *Shikwah* (The Com-
plaint) to God vividly depicts the precarious con-
ditions prevalent in the Muslim world. However,
he also composed an equally eloquent *Jawāb-i-
Shikwah* (Response to the Complaint) from God.
In this he enumerated the shortcomings of Muslims,
their internal strife, the weakness of their faith, love
of material gains and abandonment of their mission
as the causes of their downfall.

> You gave yourself to a life of ease and
> pleasure,
> As such, can you be Muslims according to
> Islamic measure?
> Contentment of Ali or riches of Uthmān,
> you have none.
> Affinity to your ancestors has long
> since gone.
>
> In their days, being Muslims, they commanded
> respect.
> By abandoning the Qur'ān you earned the
> world's disgrace.[99]

Iqbal was much perturbed and concerned seeing that the Muslims, who at one time were leading the world, had become a non-entity despite their possession of enormous potential. The causes of their downfall were identified by Iqbal in his many writings. Some causes are mentioned in the above verses but according to Iqbal some of the major causes were also asceticism in the guise of Sufism, abandonment of *ijtihād*, lack of unity and intellectual retardation.

Iqbal was very critical of the misguided popular ascetic Sufism which was prevailing in the Muslim world. It preached that the self should be annihilated in the Divine Being. It was based on the principles of Neo-Platonism and pantheistic monism. The most influential exponents of this doctrine included many Sufi poets such as Ḥāfiẓ Shīrāzī (1320–1389), who considered that the material world is unreal, it is merely an illusion. To counter this Iqbal presented the philosophy of *Khūdī* (self-assertion and self-realization) as opposed to considering this world and all its affairs worthless and useless. Thus rejecting the ides of Sufism contaminated with the *'ajamī* (non-Islamic) aspects and influences.

Iqbal was critical of the stagnation engulfing the Muslim world. As the world was progressing and new challenges and new issues were faced by the *ummah* the rigidity of the *'ulamā'* hampered progress. They remained tied up with age old laws of *fiqh* which had been formulated to deal with the issues of their time. Iqbal believed that the codification of Islamic law by an expert team of scholars was urgently needed to re-vitalize the *ummah*.

Iqbal was also concerned that the *ummah* was divided into many different nationalities, sects and racial and linguistic affiliations. Such divisions led to disintegration and conflicts. This weakened Muslims and gave opportunities for their enemies to instigate internal strife amongst them. Iqbal lamented this state of affairs and chided them:

> This people's gain and loss are common,
> as are their joys and grief.
> They have one Prophet, just one faith,
> and only one belief.
> The sanctuary of Ka'bah, God, the Qur'an,
> all one and same
> Would it be much if Muslims too were
> one? But not only in name!
> Divided into sects and factions, castes
> and creeds galore
> Is this the way towards progress? Will
> it success ensure?[100]

Finally the most serious concern of Iqbal was that Muslims were lagging behind in the field of knowledge. Once they were the leaders of the world in all branches of knowledge, when Europe was slumbering in the Dark Ages, Muslims were the torchbearers of science and technology. But gradually they became slack and lethargic and lost all interest in the pursuit of knowledge. Thus he lamented:

> You are a people that possess no worldly
> skills or knowledge
> The threat to your endangered nest, you
> neither see nor acknowledge![101]

In Iqbal's opinion the serious challenge for the Muslim *ummah* was not political subjugation but ideological submission to the West.

It is interesting to note that the first Urdu collection of his poems was called *Bāng-i-Darā – The Call of the Marching Bell* to wake up the *ummah*.

17

Sufism

Abandon the monastery and act like Ḥussain
As asceticism of the monastery is nothing
but affliction and grief.
There are traces of monasticism in your
manners and *Dīn*.
This is the old age of decline of
dying nations.[102]

*I*qbal was born in a family which was attuned to
mystic leanings. His father was a pious person
with an inclination towards mysticism; he kept the
company of scholars and Sufis. Thus Iqbal grew up
amidst a family where books of such scholars as
Ibn 'Arabī (1165–1131) were read and discussed
in a study circle. Later on, Iqbal as a postgraduate
student did extensive research on Sufism and the title
of his thesis was, *The Development of Metaphysics
in Persia*. Then he became aware that the Sufism of

Ibn ʿArabī and others is a parallel religion based on Neo-Platonism, Vadantic philosophy and escapism and is in fact contrary to Islamic teachings. After deeply studying the Qurʾān he became convinced that this strand of Sufism that preaches *Waḥdat al-Wujūd* (Unity of Being) is nothing but infidelity and heresy.

There is another group of Sufis who differentiate between the Sharīʿat and Ṭarīqat that is following the apparent (*ẓāhir*) teachings of the religion as against the inner (*bāṭin*). These Sufis believe that there was an inner aspect of the Prophet's (peace be upon him) teachings which was covert from the common people. Iqbal considered this as ridiculous and without any basis. On the contrary, the Prophet's life was like an open book and there was nothing hidden. Thus, he warned: "Do not listen to him who says there is a secret doctrine in Islam which cannot be revealed to the uninitiated."[103] This also leads to asceticism and abandoning the world that is certainly against the teachings of Islam.

Iqbal illustrated that the difference between a Prophet and a mystic was that the ultimate aim of a mystic is to attain union with God while the task of the Prophet is to lead his *ummah* and accomplish his mission in the world. This he says is very well explained by the statement of Mawlana Abdul Quddūs Gangohī (1456–1537) who was an eminent mystic of the Indian sub-continent. After narrating

the story of *Mi'rāj,* he observed: "I swear by God
that if I had reached that point, I should never have
returned." On which Iqbal commented:

> In the whole range of Sufi literature it will be
> probably difficult to find words which, in a
> single sentence, disclose such an acute percep-
> tion of psychological difference between the
> prophetic and mystic type of consciousness.
> The mystic does not wish to return from the
> repose of 'unitary experience'; and even when
> he does return, as he must, his return does not
> mean much for mankind at large. The Proph-
> et's return is creative. He returns to insert
> himself into the sweep of time with a view to
> control the forces of history, and thereby to
> create a fresh world of ideals.[104]

There was yet another section of pseudo-Sufis who
exploited masses for their worldly gains. These were
sajjādah nashīn (keepers of the tombs of mystic saints)
who are out to make money from innocent devotees.
Iqbal wrote vehemently against their deceit and
treachery. In his poem *Bāghī Murīd* (*Rebel Disciple*)
he made scathing criticism of these groups of Sufis:

> Not mere gifts – compound interest these
> saints want.
> In each hair-shirt a usurer's dressed,
> Who inherits his seat of authority
> Like a crow in an eagle's old nest.[105]

The *taṣawwuf* which, in Iqbal's view, represents the
true Islamic teaching is called *Iḥsān* and is manifest
in benevolence, good acts, generosity and tolerance.
These are the traits praised by the Qur'ān and the
Sunnah. This Islamic *taṣawwuf* leads to such qualities
as *tazkiyah* (spiritual purification), *faqr* (detachment
from worldly possessions) and *istighnā* (contentment).
These qualities give strength and courage to the heart
to cope with the struggle in life successfully. Hence,
Iqbal was appreciative of such exponents of *taṣawwuf*
as Junayd and Busṭāmī and prayed that their qualities
may be bestowed on Muslims:

> No wonder if the Muslims gain
> Their ancient glory once again –
> Sanjar's splendour pomp and state,
> The piety and *faqr* of Junayd and Busṭāmī-
> the mystics great.[106]

Aḥmad Sanjar (1085–1157) was the Seljuq ruler of
Khorasan from 1097 until 1118 then he became the
Sultan of the Seljuq Empire, which he ruled until his
death in 1157. Iqbal is referring to the pomp and
glory of that period and wished that the Muslim
ummah could again attain that past splendour.
Abu-l-Qāsim al-Junayd of Baghdad (835–910) was
a celebrated mystic and one of the most famous of
the early Sufis of Islam. He is a central figure in the
spiritual lineage of many Sufi orders. Junayd taught
in Baghdad throughout his lifetime and was an

important figure in the development of Sufi doctrine. Abū Yazīd Ṭayfūr Bin ʿĪsā Bin Surūshān al-Basṭāmī (d.874–5 or 848–9) commonly known as Bāyazīd Basṭāmī was an eminent Sufi saint, from north-central Iran who is renowned for his piety. Iqbal has presented them as the real representatives of Islamic *tasawwuf*.

18

The Individual and Society

A branch that gets detached from its tree in autumn,
A spring shower will not make it green.
Forever it will remain in autumn
It has no relationship with the tree or its branches.
Autumn is prevailing in your garden now;
Flowers are withering and droopy
The singing birds have all departed
Leaving the shady trees deserted.
Take heed from the broken branch
As you are naïve of the laws of nature.
Keep steady relationship with the *millat*
Remain attached to the tree and hope for
the spring.[107]

A branch that gets detached from the tree during autumn cannot cannot benefit from the season of spring just as an individual will only prosper within society. This simile explains that although the Muslim *ummah* is passing through an age of decline, the advice to Muslims is to remain attached with the *ummah* and hope for its recovery.

Iqbal's philosophy of *Khūdī* stressed the importance of a person's self-esteem, self-determination and self-realization. This should not indicate that they do not believe in collectivity. It is only within society that abilities of an individual grow and shine just like a pearl, which with the protection of the shell is able to display its brightness and glamour. This point is discussed by Iqbal in his poem *Rumūz-i-Bikhudi*:

> The attachment of an individual with society
> is a blessing
> His value achieves excellence through society.
> Whenever possible be a companion of society,
> It is the assembly of nobles that is graceful.
> An individual receives respect from society
> Society gets organization from individuals.[108]

Allah no doubt, taught Adam necessary knowledge and gave him guidance to live on earth and this knowledge is transmitted through one generation to succeeding generations. It is true that it is an individual with their creative intuition that makes new discoveries and inventions. However, this knowledge only flourishes by virtue of the mutual consultation, criticism and validation of other human beings. Such a cumulative advance in human knowledge and skills is only possible through society. All knowledge must be tested against the evidence and experience of others. Iqbal stressed this point emphasizing the role of the *ummah* as its disintegration led to their degeneration. By giving the simile of a wave which is nothing outside the ocean Iqbal reminded Muslims how important it is for them to continue their collective personality.

> Your honour depends on the organization
> of the *millat*,
> When this organization departs, you
> became disgraced.
> An individual subsists within the *millat*,
> He is nothing on his own.
> A wave is only in the ocean
> It is nothing outside it.[109]

Every society possesses a hidden ability to continue its existence against all odds. There are some positive forces within it which try to steer it back to the right course. Iqbal has alluded to this in his paper *The Muslim Community*:

> ... just as an individual organism, in a state of disorder, sometimes unconsciously sets up within itself forces which tend to its health, so a social organism, under corroding influences of destructive forces may sometimes call into being counteracting forces – such as the

appearance of an inspiring personality, the birth of a new ideal, or a universal religious reform – which tend to restore its original vitality...[110]

Thus, Iqbal was always hopeful that if society is based on positive values it has the latent ability to revitalize itself.

The cement that bonds Islamic society together is mutual love and affection. The Prophet (peace be upon him) said that Muslims are like a body: if one part aches, the whole body feels the pain. It is a caring society in which the poor and needy are looked after. There is respect for elders and mercy for the young. There is hospitality for guests and strangers. There is compassion for the sick and down-trodden. There is participation in marriages and funerals. There is respect for education and knowledge and there is modesty in all affairs.

19

Ijtihād

To remain fearful of the new,
Insisting on the old ways.
It is the hardest decision to make
In the life of nations.[111]

*I*qbal believed that Islam is a universal religion and
has a natural and evolutionary system of progression.
Its teachings are not confined to a particular age or
country. God is Lord of all worlds and the Prophet
(peace be upon him) was sent as a Messenger for
the entire world and for all times to come. The
guidance given in the Qur'ān should be seen in
this universal and timeless perspective. Hence the
guidance given should be interpreted and evolved
to meet the changing needs. It has the flexibility to
meet the requirements of society. Iqbal believed that
Islamic law is a vibrant and dynamic force which
is capable of tackling all problems faced by society.

He categorically rejected the commonly held view and said that "the closing of the gate of *ijtihād* is pure fiction".

Iqbal in his poetical works as well as in other writings dealt with the topic of *ijtihād*. It was a major theme in his *Lectures on the Reconstruction of Religious Thought in Islam*. In the first part of this he considered the reasons for the stagnation and mortification of *fiqh*. He identified three reasons: firstly, during the Abbasid period the flourishing of rationalist thought became a destabilizing force for Shari'ah and hence traditionalists *'ulamā'* kept *fiqh* inflexible and rigid. Secondly, the prevalence of Sufism which like rationalism was a wide ranging movement attracted talented people and they became unconcerned with worldly affairs and the Islamic state was governed by people of average talents, thus masses became strict followers of their own schools of *fiqh*. Finally the sacking of Baghdad in 1258 impelled the Islamic scholars to preserve the social structure rather than develop it through *ijtihād*. This led to undue reverence for past structures and *taqlīd*. Iqbal surveyed the historical developments of the revivalist movements in the ensuing centuries such as Ibn Ḥazm, Ibn Taymiyah, al-Suyūṭī and Imam Muḥammad ibn Abdul Wahhāb, he concluded that the treasury of *fiqh* needs revisiting, reassessment and reinterpretation.

In the second part he emphasized the value of development and progress and wrote:

I have no doubt that a deeper study of the enor-mous legal literature of Islam is sure to rid the modern critic of the superficial opinion that the Law of Islam is stationary and incapable of development.[112]

He was against stagnation and blindly following the earlier regulations formulated by *fuquhā'* to deal with the problems faced in different circumstances and environments. Yet he was not in favour of unbridled *ijtihād* by incompetent scholars. *Ijtihād* has to be done within the parameters set by Islam and its teachings and that there should be change while maintaining the stability. Iqbal laid down some basic and fundamental conditions which have to be followed by those who undertake *ijtihād*. Alongside expert understanding of the Qur'ān's historical background, Hadith, *Ijmaᶜ* (consensus of opinion of jurists) and *Qiyās* (analogical deduction) to solve the new problems the person should have a deep knowledge of modern scientific and technological progress as well. If such people are not available then Iqbal preferred to stick with traditionalist *'ulamā'* rather than shortsighted and narrow-minded scholars:

It is safer to stick with the gone-bye traditionalists
Than follow the *ijtihād* of short-sighted persons.[113]

Iqbal advocated revisiting Islamic law in order to make progress towards its codification. He realized that it is well-nigh impossible for one legal expert to make *ijtihād* as human affairs have now become too complex. He wanted to transfer the power of *ijtihād* from individuals to the representatives from different schools of *fiqh* in a Muslim legislative assembly where then could reach *Ijma'*. In this way the dormant spirit of life in the Islamic legal system could be revitalised.[114]

20

Khūdī
(Self-Respect, Ego)

The hidden secret of *khūdī* is *Lā ilāha illal Lāh*
Khūdī is a sword and its blade is *Lā ilāha illal Lāh*.[115]

This law of breath is like a sword.
Khūdī is its sharpness

Khūdī is the secret of life;
It is the world's awakening.[116]

The luminous point whose name is *khūdī*
Is the spark of life beneath our dust.[117]

*K*hūdī is the most pervasive concept found in Iqbal's
poetical and other works. It is the recurrent theme
throughout his philosophy of life. Although in Per-
sian and Urdu literature the word *khūdī* has been

used to mean vanity, pomp, and arrogance, Iqbal used this word extensively and gave it a dignified meaning. Explaining the meaning of *Khūdī* he said:

> Ethically the word *khūdī* means (as used by me) self-reliance, self-respect, self-confidence, self-preservation, even self-assertion when such a thing is necessary, in the interests of life and the power to stick to the cause of truth, justice, duty, etc., etc., even in the face of death.[118]

Iqbal's main criticism was directed against concepts of self-denial and self-abasement found in the mystical experiences of the Sufis or Vedanta philosophy in Hinduism as well as in European idealism.

Iqbal composed his Persian *Mathnawī Asrār-i-Khūdī* (The Secrets of *Khūdī*) to put forward his message to the slumbering Muslim nations. Although Iqbal gave positive meaning to *khūdī*, centuries of Sufi belief that the self should be annihilated in the Divine Being meant that Muslims could not easily accept this new philosophy. Iqbal's outspoken and scathing criticism of Sheikh Muḥy-al-Dīn Ibn al-'Arabī's (1165–1240) doctrine of *Waḥdat al-Wujūd* (Unity of Being) as well as Sufi poets like Khawjā Ḥāfiẓ Shīrāzī (1320–1389) stirred up much criticism. However, he was able to convince his critics that his is the clarion call to wake the Muslim *ummah* from slumber and inactivity. They should take up the challenges of submission, slavery, ignorance and depravity to shape their own destiny. He believed as the *khūdī* of an individual strengthens and rejuvenates he will attain respect and prestige.

Iqbal identified three stages to train and develop *khūdī*. First stage is submission to the Creator. Obedience to the will of God enhances the human personality. This means following the obligations placed on an individual by the Sharicah. The second stage is following the path of Islam which creates order and discipline as well as qualities of sacrifice and compassion in one's life. Finally, the third stage is the vice-regency of man on earth as this was the purpose for which man was created. Allah gave Adam all the knowledge and guidance that was necessary for him and his wife to act as vice-regents. Human beings should live in peace and harmony and use earth's resources for society's betterment in complete submission to the will of God. According to Iqbal, *khūdī* creates self-respect and self-reliance in a human being. Instead of depending on others for fulfilling his needs, a person struggles and uses his potential to achieve success. This is a message often repeated by Iqbal that it is through self-realization and self-knowledge that human beings can control all forces of nature and create their own destiny. This life is just the stepping stone on the road to eternity. This world is not the destination but the first step of *khūdī*.

When one has fully accomplished all the stages of *khūdī* then one has achieved self-cognition, self-respect and self-reliance. When the final stage is

reached one attains self-satisfaction. In Qur'ānic ter-
minology this is called *nafs al-muṭma'innah*.[119] This
is the stage where a servant acquires supreme felicity.
He is in control of all his faculties and has made them
subservient to his Creator. Thus, he reaches a status
where Allah accepts whatever he asks:

> Raise your *khūdī* to such a height that
> before any decree is enforced
> Allah asks His servant what is his desire?[120]

In his philosophy of *khūdī* Iqbal gave great empha-
sis on the individual personality. This created the
impression that he is in denial of collectivity. To
dispel this impression, he wrote *Rumūz-i-Bikhudi*
(The Mystery of Selflessness) in which he identifies
the basis of the *millat* or *ummah* as the development
and progression of the human personality. This is
based on the Qur'ān and the *Risālah* (Messengership)
of the Prophet (peace be upon him). Iqbal's call was
to uplift the *ummah* from its depression and state
of disarray after the demise of the *Khilāfah* and to
enthuse Muslims with dynamism and conviction.
Thus he wrote:

> Extinguishing of hope is preparation
> for death
> Life is established by the call of "Do not
> Despair".[121]

Iqbal here is quoting the Qur'ānic verse: "Do not despair of Allah's Mercy".[122] His message for the Muslim *ummah* was self-reliance and struggle and to change their situation. His call was echoing the following Qur'ānic verse:

> Verily never will Allah change the condition of a people until they change it with in their own souls.[123]

Iqbal urges the Muslim nations to use their inner resources and to make a place for themselves in this world. This according to him was the remedy for uplifting the Muslims. Just like an individual, the nation should create a consciousness of *khūdī* and preserve its identity.

Iqbal's concept of *Khūdī* as he expounded in his works, is the all-embracing call to adhere to the path of Islam. This is the way of self-recognition, self-assertion and self-fulfilment in acquiring Divine pleasure and felicity.

21

Bikhūdī

An individual's association with community
is a blessing
His mettle reaches highest perfection
through community.[124]

An individual subsists only through community
otherwise he is a nonentity.
A wave exits within the ocean otherwise it
does not exit.[125]

*I*qbal in his *Asār-i-Khūdī* (Secrets of Self) published
in 1915 laid great emphasis on the importance of
selfhood, self-realization and self-assertion. Thus,
motivating Muslims to leave the life of ease and
res-ignation to take up the challenges of the modern
age with courage and determination. This may have
created a false impression that Iqbal is neglecting
the role of society and collectivism. To dispel this

impression Iqbal wrote another poem entitled *Rumūz-i-Bikhūdī* (*Mysteries of Selflessness*) in 1918 which complements the emphasis on the self in *Asrār-i-Khūdī*. *Rumūz-i-Bikhudi* is addressed to the Muslim world. Its main theme is the ideal community, Islamic ethical and social principles and the relationship between the individual and society. In this Iqbal has attempted to balance the needs of the individual and his community as they are reflections of each other. In order to integrate an individual in the community they should be strengthened and developed as this development will cultivate the communal ego. Thus, by living in a community and having contact with others one learns to accept the limitations of one's freedom and understands the meaning of love. Our ethical values require the existence of others. It is only through mutual interaction that moral response and ethical action, if required, can be taken. It cannot be practised in a vacuum. It is impossible for love, charity, justice and sacrifice for example to be realised unless there are other humans to be loved, to be charitable to and just to, to assist and rescue through sacrifice. Muslim communities must ensure to preserve the communal tradition.

Although an individual should have free will to help him develop, it is the community in which his personality takes shape; he learns from the experiences of others and makes his own contributions for further advancement. Thus Iqbal explains this relationship between an individual and society in *Rumūz-i-Bikhūdī* as:

> Individual and nation are reflections
> of each other
> As the thread and the pearl or
> galaxy and star.
> An individual gains respect from
> the nation
> And a nation gets organization from
> individuals.
> An individual unless loses himself in
> community
> He is like a drop seeking the vastness
> of an ocean.[126]

As an Islamic poet Iqbal considered that the salvation of mankind lays in accepting the Islamic tenants: the articles of faith. Hence, he discussed *Tawḥīd* (Oneness of God) and *Risālah* (the Messengership of the Prophet Muhammad – peace be upon him). These pillars of Islam form the basis of community. He specifically mentioned the tragic events of Karbala and the martyrdom of Imam Ḥussain as this event epitomized the struggle of good and evil. It will remain a reminder of the suppression of evil until eternity. To fulfill the demand of selflessness there must be equality and brotherhood in the community. Thus an individual has to be strengthened before his integration into the community. Being in a community places limitations on him but he has to learn that these restrictions are in fact guaranteeing his freedom and he should have the capacity to forgo his individual ego for the sake of communal ego. Iqbal very carefully explains that the basis of community is not country but belief. The Muslim community must ensure discipline in their lives and must therefore preserve their communal tradition. It is in this context that Iqbal sees the vital role of women, who as mothers are hugely influential in inspiring values in their children. In this respect he presented Fāṭima al-Zahrā, the daughter of the Prophet (peace be upon him), as the model of Muslim womanhood and in the way in which she raised such children, Ḥasan and Ḥussain.

> So the flower of Ḥussain blooms from
> your branch
> The tidings of spring will come to your
> garden.[127]

In summary we see that in the West there is great emphasis on the freedom of an individual and his fundamental rights. Overemphasis on these led to the Marxist revolution which led to the tyranny of collectivism and the suppression of the individual's rights. Islam presents a balanced way of life where rights of both the individual and society are well defined and there is no oppression and suppression on either side.

22

Faqr

There is a *faqr* that teaches the hunter
to be a prey;
There is another that opens the secrets of
mastery over the world.
There is a *faqr* that is the root of needfulness
and misery among nations;
There is another that turns mere dust into elixir.
There is the *faqr* of Shabbīr (Ḥussain) which
leads to sovereignty
The real legacy of a Muslim is the
Shabbīrism treasure.[128]

*F*aqr is a recurrent theme in Iqbal's poetry. *Faqr* is usually translated as poverty, but for Iqbal it represents self-sufficiency and contentment. It shuns all trappings of power and fame. Another word he has used for *faqr* is of course *faqīr* which comes from the same root and is often translated as beggar. He also used *darwish* and *qalander* which convey a similar meaning. These words encompass traits such as *istighnā* (self-sufficiency), sacrifice, patience, humility and courage. The eminent historical figures that embody these virtues were praised by Iqbal and they include such personalities as Abū Dharr, ʿAlī ibn Abū Ṭālib, Ḥussain ibn ʿAlī, Salmān al-Farsī and Junayd al-Baghdadi.

As *faqr* teaches detachment from worldly pleasures and a life of ease and comfort, it has some similarities with monasticism. Iqbal took great pains to explain the difference between them. Thus in the poem quoted above Iqbal has presented a comparative study of *faqr* and monasticism. One teaches submission and renunciation of the world while real *faqr* teaches mastery over the forces of nature. Thus instead of living in misery and hardship the *faqr* explains the secrets of the sciences. The epitome of such *faqr* was the life of Ḥussain, whose pet name was Shabbir, which Iqbal wants Muslims to emulate.

Iqbal's emphasis and encouragement to adopt a life of *faqr* is based on the teachings of the Qurʾān and the Sunnah. In *Sūrah al-Fāṭir* Allah declares: "O Mankind! You are poor and needy while Allah is Self-Sufficient and Immensely Praiseworthy." (35: 15) Man's poverty and neediness before his Creator is never humiliation for him. He should always be conscious of his utter dependence on Allah for all his needs and not dependent on anyone else. He should consider that God is the real source of power and wealth hence he relies on Him for help and provision.

If one does this then poverty becomes the door to richness. As Junyad al-Baghdadi has said: "Richness is no more than the final, perfect degree of poverty."[129]

Whilst addressing a gathering of Muslim youths, Iqbal described the brilliance of past Muslims who taught culture and civilization. Then he quoted a hadith: "*Faqr* is my pride." Indicating that despite their pomp and glory, they gave poverty and contentment pride of place.

> *Al-Faqr Fakhrī*[130] even in the glory of
> authority existed:
> "Why would the beautiful face need
> beautifying and cosmetics."[131]
> Even in poverty these men of God were
> so high minded
> That the rich could not avoid charity for
> beggar's fear.
> In short what should I tell you what
> these wanderers were?
> They were world conquerors, world rulers,
> world administrators and world adorners.[132]

According to Iqbal *faqr* is not to rely on apparent resources. They should be disregarded and one should remain unconcerned with wealth and worldly goods. This attitude should create neither apprehension or fear nor dismay or helplessness. *Faqr* indeed is a valuable treasure which Muslims have inherited from the Prophet (peace be upon him).

There is a whole section on *faqr* in *Pas Che Bāyad Kurd Ae Aqwām-i-Sharq*! (*That You Should Be the Strategy O Nations of the East!*). Iqbal composed this long poem during an illness whilst staying in Bhopal. In this he attempted to explain *faqr* in great detail covering more than seventy verses. In this poem Iqbal urges Muslims to embrace the article of faith (*La Allāh illal Allāh*) and make complete submission with purity of heart, remain courageous and face all calamities with bravery. This is the inheritance of the Prophet (peace be upon him) and they are his protectors. This in fact is the essence of *faqr*.

Iqbal not only preached the importance of *faqr* but his practical life is the testimony that he practiced *faqr* throughout his life. He was an outstanding barrister qualified from the UK.

However, he only took a few cases, enough for him and his family's subsistence.

Iqbal was very sensitive and self-respecting, with high principles that he did not compromise. So when he was sent a cheque for one thousand rupees by Sir Akbar Hydari (1869–1941), the Chief Minister of Hyderabad, Deccan with a note that this sum is being sent from the treasury of Nizam of Hyderabad which is under my administration. It was implied that this was a personal favour. Iqbal promptly returned the cheque with a poem in which he said:

> The dignity of *faqr* would not like me to
> accept it
> When it was said it's the charity from his
> high office.[133]

23

Conviction

O Ignorant! Acquire conviction, as conviction
Provides that strength in poverty that overpowers
the monarchy.[134]

The clash between faith and reason is not new. It has plagued Western civilization for the last several centuries. But for Muslims the twentieth century was the age of scepticism when old religious beliefs and values were eroded. Materialism is the viral disease which has engulfed modern civilization. It has created love of carnal and sexual desires and a craving for quick profit. The Muslim *ummah* was not immune from these afflictions. The Muslim world was in turmoil with the impact of Western civilization and scientific discoveries. Thus instead of warmth of faith, piety and certainty Muslims are now devoid of these virtues. Muslims, though convinced about their faith often suffer from lingering doubts which prevent them from committing themselves wholeheartedly to the cause. They became doubtful of their beliefs as their senses could not perceive them. Iqbal with his insight and acumen grasped the malady that was prevalent in Muslim society. For the revival of the Muslim *ummah*, Iqbal was convinced that *yaqīn* (conviction) is needed to overcome the difficulties Muslims face. Seeing the utter despair engulfing Muslims at the turn of the 20th century when almost all Muslim nations were under colonial rule, he preached the concept of *khūdī*, which means self-recognition, self-reliance, self-respect and self-confidence. Iqbal wanted this to be reinforced with conviction.

One of the long poems at the end of Iqbal's first Urdu collection, *Bāng-i-Darā* is entitled *Ṭulu'-i-Islām* (*The Rise of Islam*). Iqbal was a realist and assessed the situation of the Muslim *ummah* with intense interest and he was convinced that the revival of the *ummah* was possible. He was optimistic that the change in the fortune of the *ummah* would happen soon, so in this poem Iqbal provided the guidance to get the *ummah* prepared for the task which was assigned to it.

> Your heart concealed the secret of
> life, disclose it.
> Relate the ups and downs of life to
> Muslims.
> You're the hand and tongue of the
> expressions of God

Cultivate certainty as you are
overwhelmed by doubt.
The conviction of a Muslim in the
abode of doubt
Is like the lamp of a hermit in the dark
night of the desert.
When this fireball of dust acquires
certainty
It also acquires the wings of Gabriel.
In slavery nothing is effective neither
swords nor planning,
If there is the love of certainty the
chains get cut off.
Firm conviction, constant action and
Love as conqueror of the world:
These are the swords for men in the
struggle of life.
Certainty of individuals is the wealth
fot building a nation
This is the only strength which shapes
the destiny of nations.[135]

Thus through this long poem Iqbal kept reiterat-
ing the importance of conviction as for him that is
the only weapon which will overwhelm the enemy.
Iqbal also warns that conviction requires great cour-
age and stamina as well as sacrifice and it is not an
easy undertaking. It requires firm faith to give the
ultimate sacrifice.

Conviction is sitting in a fire like
Ibrāhīm.
Conviction is devotion to Allah and
self-realization
Listen, O prisoner of Modernism!
Uncertainty is worse than slavery.[136]

Here Iqbal presents the faith and conviction of
Prophet Ibrāhīm (peace be upon him) as an excellent
example as he courageously faced the wrath of
the ruling monarch and without hesitation was
prepared to be thrown in the fire. Conviction means
complete devotion and absorption in the love of
God. Hence, those who are captivated with the spell
of modern civilization and culture that has resulted
in scepticism, they are worse than slaves as they have
no control over their affairs.

24

Education

May God confront you with a stormy
situation?
As there are no violent waves in the
ocean of your life.
For you the book is indispensible,
As you are just a reader not its master.[137]

*I*qbal in the above quatrain addressed to a student
educated in a modern school, admonishes him for
becoming a passive receptor. Knowledge has not
stirred in him curiosity and critical faculties. So he
prays that knowledge creates in him questioning and
turbulence and leads him to creativity and action.

During Iqbal's time two parallel systems of
education were running. One was devoted to
traditional religious education in which, the Qur'ān,
Hadith and Islamic subjects were taught using the
old *Dars-i-Nizāmī* curriculum.[138] The other system

was introduced by the British whose purpose was to prepare students for the lower ranks of civil service so that they could administer its Indian colony. Iqbal was critical of both these systems, as these do not develop a dynamic and all-rounded personality to lead the world. For Iqbal education should play a decisive role in uplifting a society and to lead it to a higher pinnacle of achievement. The educational system shapes individuals and through them the society in which they live. Iqbal laid great stress on internal training and his poetry has explicitly dealt with moral, religious and national issues. For Iqbal the objective of education should be to maximize the potential of an individual. It should prepare a student to lead an active and purposeful life rather than living passively. Thus education should develop the creative faculty and it should be primarily a dynamic and visionary process through which latent talents are nurtured. It is something which equips a person to discover new realms and avenues of art and science by opening new horizons of knowledge. This should inspire a person to be optimistic and give him faith in the future development of the human race. Thus, lamenting the paucity of knowledge Iqbal writes in his poem *Tarbīat* (*Training*):

Life is one thing, knowledge is something else.
Life is the burning of one's liver, while
knowledge is consuming one's brain.

Knowledge is endowed with wealth,
power and pleasure
But the problem is one gets lost and can't
trace oneself.
Knowledgeable are many but those with
vision are few
No wonder your bowl is empty and bare.
The ways of the sheikh of the *maktab*[139]
could not open up your heart.
How can a matchstick light up an
electric lamp?[140]

Again Iqbal was critical of *maktabs'* teachers as they
did not teach independent thinking and critical anal-
ysis. He gave the example of an eaglet that should be
taught to soar high but instead was taught to grovel
in the dust.

O Lord, I have a complaint against teachers
for they are teaching the eaglets to grovel
in the dust.[141]

In his criticism of *madrasah* education, Iqbal time
and again made very sarcastic remarks to voice his
concern and utter disgust about this system which
by rote learning throttles all initiative in students.

Madrasah teachers have strangulated
your throat
So how can the chant of Lā ilāha illā Allāh
emanate?

I am saddened by the affairs of the *madrasah*
and monastery
There is no life, no love, no enlightenment
nor insight.[142]

He also directly addressed the administrators and
teachers of such *madrasas* imploring them to incul-
cate in their students the ideas of self-realization and
self-confidence.

O Sheikh! Discard these reclusive
ways of your monastery
And grasp what my morning lament
denotes.
May God preserve the youth you guide.
Teach them how to break away from
the constraints
And teach them how to guard their 'Self'.
They are heartbroken because of
centuries of subjugation.
Think of some cure for their distraught
sight – their development.[143]

The problem with Western education was even
more disastrous as it teaches separation of religion
from worldly affairs. It advocated secularism and
materialism.

We were happy by the progress of our
youth
However, the happiness is tinged with
sorrow.

We thought that education will bring
prosperity
We didn't know that it will bring
apostasy as well.[144]

Iqbal considered that the Arabic word *'Ilm* which
translated as knowledge is more comprehensive and
includes in its ambit religious, material as well as
spiritual aspects. For Iqbal knowledge and training
should be combined to train an individual as mere
bookish knowledge is not that worthwhile.

In the concluding part of *Bāng-i-Darā* entitled
Zarīfānah (*Humorous*) Iqbal, in a lighter vein, has
contrasted the courteous relationship between teacher
and pupil in an Islamic school with that of the business-
like attitude developed by the Western educational
system.

There was a time when in exchange
for the teacher's service
One wanted the gift of the heart be
presented!
Times have changed so much that the
pupil after the lesson
Says to the teacher: "May I have the
bill please?"[145]

25

Science

Who has carried off Love's valiant sword?
An empty scabbard remained in Knowledge's hand,
O *Saqī*[146]![147]

*T*here are extensive uses of symbols in Iqbal's poetry.
He used ordinary words and assigned them specific
meanings. In the above verse by 'Knowledge' Iqbal
refers to that knowledge which one acquires through
one's senses. In other words it is scientific knowledge
which explains physical laws. While Love in Sufi
terminology represents love of God. Iqbal is lamenting
the fact that once science was under the scrutiny of
religion and its sword was dismantling the fraudulent
ideas and ideologies but now that sword has been
carried off by someone and its scabbard is empty.
Although Iqbal here did not identify the culprit,
it is of course the Western theories which deny the

existence of God. Western scientific knowledge as-
sumes a godless universe and bases all biological,
physical and psychological sciences on observations
and experimentations. Regretfully the Muslim world
also followed the West blindly copying their scientific
theories.

Iqbal has recorded these divergent views between
Knowledge and Love in the form of a dialogue in
Payām-i-Mashriq.

Science boasts that my eyes encompass the whole
universe and everything is under my control. I am
only concerned with this world and I do not indulge
in metaphysics. My music evolves hundreds of songs
and I display all the secrets openly, so that anyone
can benefit from them. Love responded by enumer-
ating the havocs caused by harmful inventions like
ammunitions, bombs and poisonous gases which
caused untold devastations in the world. With the
cognizance of God both Love and Knowledge pro-
gressed together (as during the Muslim period of sci-
entific inventions). Allah's Light guided us but when
Science left that path the Light became fire. Finally
Love suggested:

Let us make the world a rose garden
And rejuvenate the old world as young.
Come and take a particle from my
heart's affliction
Let us create underneath the sky an
everlasting paradise.

We were together since eternity
We are part of the same song of low and
high tunes.[148]

It should not be construed that Iqbal was against the
progress of science and technology and the benefits
they bestow on humanity. The Qur'ān has repeat-
edly stressed that man should observe the universe
and the different natural phenomena all around
him. However, Iqbal was against the one-sided blind
following of scientific inventions disregarding their
harmful effects on human beings and the environ-
ment, thus neglecting life's spiritual dimension and
basing everything on materialism. Iqbal rejects the
claim of those who consider that science can com-
prehensively study all human affairs. He believed
that science was limited as man also has a spiritual
dimension, which is beyond the reach of science.

Distracted are your eyes in myriad ways
Distracted is your reason in many pursuits.[149]

However, if your aim and intention by studying the
universe is to unravel the marvels of God's creation
and discover their beauty and utility then your
efforts will be fruitful.

This universe does not hide its secrets
Every particle is beaming with revelation.
You can observe some different aspects
of the world

If your yearning eyes are accompanied by
your insight.
If you do not possess such yearning eyes
Your existence is a disgrace for your heart
and mind.[150]

According to Iqbal if one studies the universe in the
light of faith in God then they will be able to draw
the correct conclusions from their observations and
their insight will guide them all the way.

That Knowledge is an iconoclast[151] of his
own idols,
Whose heart and mind are made companions
by God.
Such knowledge is short sightedness which
does not embrace
And illuminate the surroundings for Mūsā
and unveil
the philosophical observations for the wise.[152]

In conclusion it can be said that Iqbal was of the
view that it is dangerous to depend solely on science
for guidance and regulation in life. There should be
passion and not cold intellectualism. To this end one
needs the warmth of love and intuition also. Natu-
ralism has given humanity an unprecedented control
over the forces of nature, but has robbed it of faith
in its own future. There needs to be the guiding hand
of faith to lead humanity to a balanced life.

26

Fine Art

O Man of Vision! Pleasure of beauty is appreciable
Yet what if the sight doesn't discern reality!
The purpose of art is to enkindle eternal passion
What is the point of a fleeting spark!
Lyric of a poet or a melody of a singer
If the garden is depressed, no use is zephyr.
Nations do not rise without a miracle in the world;
You need to possess Moses's rod to strike.[153]

*F*ine art is a visual art to satisfy man's aesthetic and intellectual faculty appreciating its beauty and meaningfulness. The perception of aesthetic qualities requires a refined judgement, this is how a person develops good taste which differentiates fine art from popular art and entertainment. In every art form there is a human desire for beauty and the ultimate purpose of this is the quest for beauty that is the true love of the Creator which evokes warm longing.

For Iqbal this desire for beauty or love of God is truly manifested in The Mosque of Cordoba which he visited in the 1930s. The poem he composed on that occasion is the masterpiece of his poetry. The architecture of the Mosque captivated his heart and the sentiments he expressed are full of ecstasy. Here are just a few verses:

O Harem of Cordoba!
To love that is eternal;
Never waning, never fading.
Just the material these pigments, bricks
and stones;
This harp, these words and sounds, just
the expression.
The miracle of art springs from the lifeblood
of the artist!

A droplet of the lifeblood
Transforms a piece of dead rock into a
living heart;
An impressive sound into a song of
solitude,
A refrain of rapture or a melody of mirth.
The aura you exude illuminates the heart.
My plaint kindles the soul.
You draw hearts to the Presence Divine.

Incomplete are all creations
Without the lifeblood of the creator,

Soulless is the melody
Without the lifeblood of the maestro.[154]

Iqbal concludes the poem with a message in the last
verse that nothing in any art-form could be achieved
without struggle and even poetry needs lifeblood to
achieve perfection.

The sturdy and magnificent architecture of the
Masjid Quwwat al-Islam, which is famous for its
magnificent minaret – Quṭb Minār, Delhi, evokes
different sentiments in Iqbal.

Why Muslims should not be ashamed
As their slavery has made them like a
brittle glass.
Prayers of those is worthy of your
splendour
Whose Call for Prayers enrages battle
between good and evil. [155]

Thus, Iqbal is implying that only those who possess
valour, determination and courage are entitled to
pray in this grand and lofty mosque.

There is a section in *Ḍarb-i-Kalīm* in which Iqbal
touched upon all art forms and discussed what is
desirable and what should be ignored. With regard
to music, Iqbal wanted that melody which inspires
the soul by freeing oneself from anxiety and fear and
enthuses the downtrodden to dream of acquiring a
higher status in life. This uplifting quality of music

has much to be appreciated. In contrast to this there is another form of music popularized in Sufi circles which teaches annihilation and led to forgetfulness and oblivion. This is to be avoided. Same is the case with dance which may agitate the baser instincts.

As in all other aspects of life, Iqbal is critical of following the Western tradition in all art forms. He particularly resented the adoption of the Western school of painting. He lamented that the painters who possess talent and can create paintings reflecting their own culture and traditions are blindly following Western art.

For Iqbal it was essential that man should keep his individuality and preserve his *khūdī* (self-realization and self-preservation). Hence he was critical of art forms like theatre and cinema in which actors submerged their personalities and assumed the roles of others thereby losing their own identity.

Finally, addressing all artists, poets, dramatists, writers, painters and musicians he lamented and admonished them as they did not faithfully portray the realities of life, they did not awaken the soul as they are only concerned with the baser emotions.

O the poets, painters and writers of India!
Oh Pity! Woman is in possession of your nerves.[156]

27

Women

Existence of a woman makes the universe colourful,
Her music unravels life's inner burning.
Her handful lump of dust is more honourable
than the Pleiades
As all honour is a small casket of its hidden pearl.
Although she did not compose Plato's *Dialogues*
Yet it's from her flame that Plato's flare gets charged.[157]

The status of women and the role they play in the family and in the community is vital for the creation of a healthy and smooth running household and society. The disparity between the rights and duties of genders is responsible for disruption and anarchy. Islam equitably defined these roles. While a man as the head of the family is responsible for looking after his wife and children and providing for their upkeep, a woman's role is to manage the household and bring up the children to the best of her ability.

Thus, man and woman perform their duties within their domains. This does not mean that a woman is confined within her home. On the contrary women are free to participate in the economic, social and political affairs of society. Illustrating this point Iqbal in the above poem mentioned that though Plato's[158] mother did not write a notable philosophical treatise like *Dialogues*, she gave birth and brought up plato to produce such a work.

Iqbal in several poems in the section on Woman in *Darb-i-Kalīm* highlighted her role in society. While criticizing the limitless freedom and disequilibrium that is now plaguing the West, Iqbal blames not the women but Western society for not understanding the psychology of a woman.

> This is not the fault of the woman in creating this havoc
> Even the moon and Pleiades will vouchsafe her integrity.
> The chaos appearing in the Western society prevails
> As man is a simpleton and poor fellow does not understand the woman.[159]

The emancipation of women was a debated issue during Iqbal's life time. Although he was noncomittal he knew that this would create problems in society as sexual anarchy and shamelessness was already prevalent in the West. However, this does not mean that he was against women playing a positive role in society and being educated and trained. However, if such education as was prevalent in the West, teaching women to abandon motherhood and become manlike then this will be disastrous. In a poem *Woman and Education* Iqbal wrote:

> If Western culture leads to the death of
> motherhood
> Then it is the death knell for the human race.
> If by education a woman becomes a non-
> woman
> Then the learned reckons this education as
> death.
> If women's school remain unaware of religion
> Then this knowledge and training is
> death for love and affection.[160]

For Iqbal motherhood is the most pious and high ranking status for a woman. This leads to stability and firmness in social relations. In *Rumūz-i-Bikhūdī* Iqbal has discussed this issue at length under the heading *"The Meaning of the Preservation of the human race is Motherhood and the Preservation and Respect of Motherhood is Islam."* In the following few verses he has discussed the importance of motherhood:

> *Millat* is just to respect the wombs,
> Otherwise the deeds of life are
> just futile.

It is from motherhood that life is throbbing.
It is motherhood that reveals the mysteries
of life.
My stream is in hectic motion because of
motherhood.
Thus creating waves, the whirlpools and
bubbles.
Mothers are the protectors of the expression
of brotherhood
Mothers are the strength of the Qur'ān
and *millat*.[161]

Finally, Iqbal presents Fāṭimah al-Zahra, the daughter of the Prophet (peace be upon him) as a role model of motherhood for Muslim women.

She was the harvest of the well-sown field
Of self-surrender, to all mothers, she
The perfect pattern, Fāṭimah, the chaste.[162]

To Iqbal the life and character of Fāṭimah (her honorific name in the above verse was Batūl – chaste one) is not only the perfect model of Muslim womanhood, rather it is worth imitating by all womankind. According to Iqbal, it is a mother who is mainly responsible for instilling good virtues in her children and it is a mother who is the real builder of good character and great personality in a community's children. Iqbal spoke of the mother in high esteem:

The Character of children comes from
their mothers,
The essence of truth and purity comes
from their mothers.[163]

28

Youth

The youth who dare to reach the stars
Are the ones I love indeed.[164]

Youth are the future of every nation. They are the ones who make efforts to preserve and carry forward the culture and civilization of a nation. Thus, Iqbal wanted to motivate Muslim youth to get ready to contribute their due role in the community's character building. Youth form important addressees of Iqbal's poetry as he considered them a symbol of hope and the bright future for the nation. However, he was disappointed to observe that instead of pursuing the acquisition of knowledge and persevering in the task of nation-building, the youth are enjoying a life of comfort and ease. He was dismayed and expressed his frustration in the following verses addressed to a young person:

Your sofas are from Europe, your fine
carpets from Iran;
My eyes weep blood seeing such pampered
ways among youth.
No use the pomp of Khosrow, nor rank
or high office
You are not brave like 'Alī nor content
like Salmān.

Don't seek contentment in the glittering
modern world
The joy and greatness of a Muslim lie in
contentment with Islam.

When the eagle spirit is awakened
in the youth,
It sees its destination in the starry skies.
Despair not, for despair is decline of
knowledge and wisdom
A believer's hopes are among the
confidants of God.

Your abode is not on the dome of a
royal palace;
You are an eagle and should live on
the rocks of mountains.[165]

Iqbal's advice to youth was not to be tempted by
the glitter of worldly goods and live a luxurious life
like Khosrow (496–579) an Iranian king, instead he

wanted them to live a life of contentment and brav-
ery by following the example of 'Alī ibn Abū Ṭālib
and Salmān Farsī, the two eminent Companions
or just like an eagle aspiring for high altitudes and
choosing the rugged mountains rather than palatial
surroundings for a sojourn.

This was the constant theme whenever Iqbal
had a chance to address a gathering of youth with
the hope that it would arouse them from their deep
slumber. Lamenting on the lost heritage of Muslims
Iqbal wanted them to feel shameful and thus motivate
them to action. Following are some of the verses:

> O Muslim youth! Have you ever
> used your prudence?
> What was that sky of which you are
> a fallen star?
> You have no relationship with your
> ancestors:
> You just talk while they were full
> of actions,
> You are stationary while they were
> revolving.
> We have wasted the heritage of our
> ancestors;
> The sky has thrown us down from
> Pleiades to earth![166]

In *Javed Nāmah* there is an Appendix which is
entitled an "*Address to Javed*" and through him to

the young generation of Muslims. Javed was his son and through him Iqbal wanted to convey this advice to the Muslim youth. In this Iqbal deplores the outward show of piety and the neglect of the inner dimension of worship by Muslims, their backwardness in all fields of knowledge and their utter bewilderment at the glittering civilization of the West. He was grieved to see that the young generation was disenchanted, lacking conviction and vision. Thus, he offered them his advice for changing the situation.

> Among the Muslims you will seek in vain
> The faith, the ecstasy of days bygone.
> The scholars are without Qur'ānic lore;
> The Sufis, long-haired beasts and nothing more.
> The frenzy at the saints' tombs is a fraud:
> Show me a single man who drunk with God.
> As for the Muslims dazzled by the West,
> A mirage is the object of their quest.
> These men cannot at all appreciate
> Religion: they are instigators of hate.
> The privileged possess no charity:
> But in the masses there's no sincerity.
> "Distinguish men of faith from men of hate.
> Seek out a man of God for your mate."[167]

Iqbal advised them to follow the path of distinguished prophets and those who remained steadfast on this path. He asked them to take Rūmī as their guide and to acquire his burning and consuming anguish. His final words were:

> O Impatient comfort of my soul!
> May you be endowed with ecstasy.
> I am imparting to you the secret of the *Dīn*
> Even in my grave I will pray for you.[168]

Iqbal was his most eloquent when he addressed young Muslims:

> The narration of the sacred precinct, if told
> Is simple, strange and yet red in hue:
> It begins with Isma'īl, the bold
> And ends with Ḥussain, the martyr true.[169]

He presented two role models for Muslim youth providing simple lessons of devotion, honesty and commitment. Thus he summarized a young Muslim's role as that of Isma'īl and Ḥussain (peace be upon them). The Prophet Isma'īl taught that one should be prepared to sacrifice oneself in the prime of youth by obeying Allah's command disregarding one's own ambitions and aspirations. Imam Ḥussain, on the other hand, chose martyrdom fighting oppression rather than submitting to the ruler who was tarnishing the ideals of Islam. Present day youth should follow these examples and be ready to oppose and suppress oppression in their society.

29

Children

لب پہ آتی ہے دُعا بن کے تمنّا میری
زندگی شمع کی صورت ہو خدایا میری

دُور دُنیا کا مرے دَم سے اندھیرا ہوجائے
ہر جگہ میرے چمکنے سے اُجالا ہوجائے

ہو میرے دَم سے یونہی میرے وطن کی زینت
جس طرح پھول سے ہوتی ہے چمن کی زینت

زندگی ہو میری پروانے کی صورت یارّب
علم کی شمع سے ہو مجھ کو محبت یارّب

ہو مرا کام غریبوں کی حمایت کرنا

دردمندوں سے، ضعیفوں سے محبت کرنا

مرے اللہ! بُرائی سے بچانا مجھ کو

نیک جو راہ ہو، اُس راہ پہ چلانا مجھ کو

(بانگ درا، ص۴۹، ۵۰)

A CHILD'S SUPPLICATION

My longing comes to my lips as a supplication of mine.
O My God! Let my life be like a candle that shines.
May the world's darkness disappear through
this life of mine!
May everything light up with the brightness of mine!
Through me my homeland attains elegance,
As a garden through flowers attains elegance.
May the life of mine be a moth, My Lord!
That loves the lamp of knowledge, My Lord!
O God! Protect me from the evil ways,
Lead me to the path of virtuous ways.[170]

*I*qbal was a versatile poet and composed poems
covering all genres' of poetry. It was exceptional that
a poet of such calibre also successfully wrote poems
for children that made him immortal during his
lifetime. This short poem of only six verses, whose

central theme is taken from a Western poet, has become the best loved and most popular poem in the Indo-Pakistan subcontinent. Even before the Partition the poem became so popular that every Muslim child was made to learn it by heart, even now the morning assembly in all schools in Pakistan and many Muslim schools in India and Bangladesh start the day with this very appropriate prayer.

The essence of the prayer is a desire to change so that one becomes a beacon of light to brighten up the darkness of ignorance. One should become a worthy person for one's community and nation by enkindling the lamp of knowledge and by helping the poor and destitute. And finally, echoing the prayer from *Sūrah al-Fātiḥah* by seeking guidance to the right path.

Another patriotic song – *Tarāna-i-Hindī (An Ode to India)* was also very popular and could have been adopted as the Indian National Anthem had there been no partition of India. It received much praise even from Hindu leaders for the sentiments expressed in the poem. A few of its verses capture India's beauty and its distinguished history:

Best of the whole world is this land of ours.
We are its nightingales it is the garden of ours.
The highest mountain touching the sky
It is our sentinel, it is our watchman.
Greece, Egypt, Rome are all now extinct
But our fame and renown still prosper.[171]

Iqbal wrote many other poems for children. Some of them were adapted from English and the works of American poets like Tennyson, Emerson, Longfellow and others. All his poems for children are in his first Urdu Collection – *Bāng-i-Darā*. Some of the famous poems are: *Aik Makrā aur Makhī* (*A Spider and a Fly*) which teaches that flattery can lead to destruction; *Aik Pahār aur Gulehrī* (*A Mountain and a Squirrel*) which concludes as:

> Nothing is useless in the world
> Nothing is bad in God's creation.[172]

Aik Gāye aur Bakri (*A Cow and a Goat*) teaches that one should not complain without a valid reason. But the most tragic poem which is adapted from one of William Cowper's poems is the *Lament of a Bird* in which a caged bird remembers its past life enjoying the free life in a garden with its friends. His longing to join them and rejoice in a leisurely and unhindered life were beautifully depicted by Iqbal. It may be an allegorical poem depicting India under colonial rule.

In these poems Iqbal teaches children moral values and ways of living. If children read these poems they will be open to read Iqbal's other poems. Iqbal's poetry is full of the message of hope and optimism as well as the love of Islam. This could influence their way of living and they could then be able to play a major role in the development of themselves and their country.

30

Western Civilization

Your civilization will commit suicide with
its own dagger.
A nest built on a fragile branch is sure
to be doomed.[173]

Western civilization evolved over the centuries. It began to take shape by weakening the hold of Christianity. With the Reformation, the authority of the Catholic Church lost its hold in many Western European countries. The Enlightenment of the 18th century emphasized reason, analysis and individualism rather than the traditional lines of authority. It challenged the authority of institutions that were deeply rooted in society. This was followed by the scientific revolution. This included the emergence of modern science, during which developments in mathematics, physics, astronomy, biology and chemistry trans-formed views of society and nature. The theory of Evolution as propounded by Darwin (1809–1882) in the mid-nineteenth century transformed the entire outlook on human values and norms. Thus, spirituality was replaced by materialism and atheism while morality was substituted by liberalism. Then during the period of colonialism Western culture was exported to other countries around the world.

Iqbal during his three-year stay in the first decade of the twentieth century in Europe for his education gained first-hand experience by observing Western culture. He realized that materialism, pantheism and atheism had corroded spiritual values and despite all the advances in science and technology the West was still left restless and soulless. He compared it to 'an empty scabbard chased with flowery gilt' and he genuinely believed that it would eventually 'commit suicide with its own dagger'.

Iqbal concludes *Asrār-i-Khūdī* which he composed a few years after his return from Europe with a supplication, imploring that:

Let Love engaged in *Lā* be informed,
Be acquainted of the mystery of *Illā Allāh*.[174]

This refers to the first part of the Article of Faith that starts with a rejection of all false gods (*Lā ilāha*). This is followed by an affirmation of One God (*illā Allāh*). Iqbal's criticism of Western philosophers is that they only managed to reach the stage of *Lā* – denial of false gods. They proclaimed that there is no god but then failed to progress to the affirmation of *Tawḥīd* (Oneness of God). He took up this lapse of Western philosophers in several of his poems.

> The goblet of modern civilization is filled
> to the brim with the wine of *Lā*
> Pity that the cupbearer does not hold the
> glass of *Illā*.[175]

Iqbal observed that at the turn of the twentieth century, the Islamic world together with the rest of humanity was dominated by Western culture and philosophy. In the wake of Western imperialism the Muslim world was in turmoil and was unable to resist the rising tide of Western thought. Iqbal's message was that Muslims should free themselves from the mental slavery of the West and imbibe Islamic values in their lives and embark on the building of a new world order. His mature and perceptive criticism of Western thought exposed its utter hopelessness and his prescription for remedying the prevalent deviation and misguidance was to regain certainty and faith. His advice to Muslims was to capture the governance of the world to save it from its doom:

> The might of the West could not even tear
> any collar
> Though Westerners are supposed to be
> very clever.

The wine of certainty is firing the conscience
of the world
O Lord! May this fiery liquid enlighten the
Madrasah?
Everyone is waiting for the ascent of
earthly Adam
The galaxy, the stars and the azure sky.
Is this the wealth of the present age?
Bright minds, yet blackened hearts and
uncontrolled eyes!
If you are sightless then of course you
cannot see
Otherwise a *Mu'min* sets fire to the pastures
of the world.
The world assumes that Reason is the torch
that shines the way
Who knows even an insane can possess the
virtue of perception
The entire universe is the heritage of a
Mard-i-Mu'min[176]
The truth of my assertion sprang from
Lawlāk.[177,178]

Iqbal's critique of Western civilisation should be studied in its historical context. Most of Asia and Africa were then dominated by Western colonial powers. There was a quest for freedom and liberation from the materialistic and hedonistic philosophy of the West. In this respect he was echoing the thoughts of many other Western philosophers.

31

The Political System

Whether it is the majesty of monarchy or
democratic spectacle
When religion is divorced from politics
it is tyranny.[179]

Reformation in Europe in the 16th century led to
the separation of Church and State. The political
system was based on the philosophy that material
and spiritual spheres of life are two different entities.
Over the centuries the church had become deeply
involved in the political life of European countries.
This resulted in many intrigues and political ma-
nipulations. The Church also abused its power and
privileges. This led to the curtailment of the public
role of the Church. Iqbal graphically depicted this
tension between these two institutions in his poem
Church and State (Dīn wa Siyāsat):

Monasticism was the church's base
Its austere living had no room for wealth.
The priest and the king have ever
been hostile;
One has humility, the other an exalted
power.
Church and state were separated at last;
The revered priest was rendered powerless.
When church and state parted ways
forever,
It set the rule of avarice and greed.
This split is disaster both for country
and faith,
And shows the culture's blind lack of vision.
It is the miracle of a desert-dweller
The conveyance of good tidings blends
with warning.
Mankind's deliverance lies in the fact
That both Junayd and Ardashīr[180] get united.[181]

However, in Islam there is no such dichotomy. There is no separation of the spiritual and temporal aspects of life instead there is a beautiful synthesis between the two. As Iqbal had a deep knowledge of Islamic teachings and history, he did not believe that Islam was restricted only to dogmas and a set of rituals. In fact, Islam presents a complete way of life embracing personal, social, economic as well as political systems. He believed that the prime duty of an Islamic state is to provide freedom, equality and stability in society. Thus what he was advocating in the last line of the poem is unison of the spiritual life of Junayd al-Baghdadi (835–910), a famous mystic, with the political power of King Ardashir (180–242) the founder of the Sasanian Empire in Iran.

To start with, Iqbal was against the Western system of democracy which defused sovereignty amongst the masses. In Islam God is the sole Sovereign and to Him belongs "the dominion of the universe and Who has power over everything." (al-Mulk 67: 1) Iqbal echoing this Qur'ānic precept wrote:

> Sovereignty befits only to that Matchless One
> He is the real Ruler all else Āzar's idols.[182]

Āzar was the name of the Prophet Ibrāhīm's (peace be upon him) father, who carved idols in the city of Ur and refused to accept the message of *Tawḥīd* (Oneness of God) preached by his illustrious son.

For the wellbeing and welfare of humanity it is essential that power and supremacy should have a restraining influence from ethics and morality. If this does not happen then political power becomes a demon without fetters and thus creates havoc in society.

> In my view this secular politics
> Is the slave-girl of the devil, mean and
> without conscience.
> The state abandoning the Church is now free.
> The politics of the West is demons let loose.[183]

The power of the modern state is all pervasive and an individual citizen is helpless. In fact it has become a new idol which one is forced metaphorically to worship. Iqbal wanted to demolish this hypocrisy and maintain that state was an institution which should serve the individual; to raise its status to divinity is against rational thinking.

32

Nationalism

Muslims have also constructed their own sanctuary
This Āzar of civilization has carved idols of its own.
Homeland is the biggest idol among the
newly created ones
Its apparel in fact is the shroud of religion.
This idol is the product of a new civilization
In fact it is the destroyer of the Prophet's *Dīn*.
You are strengthened by the belief in *Tawḥīd*
Islam is your country and you are the
followers of the Prophet!
Then show the world the glory of the past
By demolishing this idol, O Follower of
the Prophet![184]

he first phase of Iqbal's poetry was saturated with
patriotic fervor. His first collection of Urdu poems
Bāng-i-Darā published in 1924 opens with an ode
to Himālah – the Himalayan Mountains, in which
he extols the beauty of this majestic mountain range

guarding like a sentinel the northern borders of India. The anthology also includes many poems displaying his love and affection for his motherland such as *Hindustānī Bachun kā Quamī Gīt* (*National Song for Indian Children*), *Tarāna-i-Hindī* (*National Anthem of India*), *Nayā Shivāla* (*A New Temple*) and many others. These patriotic compositions are contained in Part I of *Bāng-i-Darā* covering the period up to 1905. Love for one's country is a natural instinct which is experienced by all, but many commentators have attributed this to Iqbal's advocacy of nationalism. Perhaps during this period lines between patriotism and nationalism got blurred. There is a subtle difference between patriotism and nationalism. A patriot is proud of his country for what it does and stands for, while a nationalist is proud of his country no matter what it does; this is what led to the slogan "my country right or wrong". The first attitude creates a feeling of responsibility for the welfare of one's country while the second is a feeling of blind arrogance that often leads to conflict and war.

When Iqbal came to Europe in 1908 for his higher studies, he observed firsthand the fierce nationalism raging in Europe which ultimately led to two world wars in the last century. This idea of nation started only in the mid-nineteenth century in Europe and created bitter rivalries among different nations. As some of the European countries were also colonial powers their rivalries continued overseas. They also found it convenient to divide other countries up on the basis of nations and to create disharmony amongst them. This was particularly evident when the British and the French destroyed the Ottoman Caliphate by instigating the Arabs against the Turks and then dividing the Middle East under different nationalities: Syrian, Iraqis, Turks, Egyptian and Lebanese. Iqbal foresaw this plan of the European colonial powers and denounced nationalism in his writings.

Iqbal's stay in Europe certainly changed his outlook on world affairs and he became more *ummah* orientated. Iqbal wrote patriotic verses at the beginning. Later on he started composing poems like the *Islamic Community Song (Tarana-i-Millī)*:

> China and Arabia as well as India all
> belong to us
> We are Muslims; the whole world is our
> country.
> The leader of our caravan is the lord of Ḥijāz
> His name is a source of comfort for us.[185]

He was critical of blindly following the secular ideas which were prevailing in the West. In fact he may be echoing his own conversion to becoming a real Muslim when he wrote:

> The storm of the West has transformed
> Muslims into real Muslims
> Only the upheavals of the sea cultivate a
> pearl's beauty to perfection.[186]

Thus, in the aforementioned verses from his poem *Waṭanīat* (*Nationalism*) he bitterly criticized the territorial nationalism which he considered opposed to Islamic teachings creating dissension and dividing humanity. Here Iqbal had taken care to add a note to explain that by nationalism he meant the political ideology.

Iqbal stressed that the basis of Islam is not nationality. The Declaration of Faith by which a person becomes a Muslim creates a universal brotherhood amongst its followers. Thus even very close relations of the Prophet (peace be upon him) and dwellers of his city, of the same colour and race and who spoke the same language, did not accept Islam and became *millat-i-kufr* (community of unbelievers) while Bilāl from Abyssinia (modern Ethiopia) and Ṣuhaib from Rūm (Asia Minor) who were from different nations became part of the Muslim *ummah*. While contrasting the constitution of the Muslim *ummah* to the Western concept, Iqbal stated in his poem *Madhab* (*Religion*):

Compare not your nation on the criteria
of the West.
Special is the composition of the nation of
the Hāshmī Prophet.
Country and race are the basis of their
organization,
While the strength of the religion stabilize
yours.

If the attachment with religion were to
slip away
then organization gets lost;
And if organization departs so does
the nation![187]

In Islam there are no artificial barriers of race, colour,
languages or nationality. The only criterion for dis-
tinction is *taqwā* (God-consciousness). This precept
is reiterated by Iqbal in his writings:

Islam does not recognize the differences of
race, of caste or even sex. It is above time and
space and it is this sense that all mankind are
accepted as brothers.[188]

Iqbal thus warned those who try to create distinc-
tion between human beings on the basis of artificial
criteria that they will be destroyed.

Whoever discriminates on the basis of
colour or race would perish
Be he a tent-dwelling Turk or high
ranking Arab.
If race were to become more important
than *Dīn*
Muslims would be blown away like dust
from this world.[189]

33

Democracy

Democracy is a system of government
Where you count people and do not
weigh their ability.[190]

Refrain from the democratic system and
follow the confirmed way
Brains of two hundred asses will not
yield wisdom.[191]

*F*rom Iqbal's writing it is quite evident that he was
not in favour of the Western idea of democracy. He
did not subscribe to an unbridled mass participation
in choosing and governing a country. Although he
wholeheartedly supported the freedom of the individ-
ual and his philosophy of *khūdī* promotes self-
realization and self-expression, he was averse to the
Western democratic right of one person, one vote.
The reason for his opposition was that although in

theory democracy is there to safeguard human rights, freedom of thought, speech and action as well as to promote equality and justice, in practice it becomes tyranny of the elected few over the majority of the people. The despotism of the elected cabal exploited the masses.

It is the same old song of the Western
democratic system
In its curtain rang nothing but lyrics of
kingship.
It is the devil of despotism in the cloak
of wooden feet
You think it is the beautiful fairy of
democracy.
The legislative assembly, the reforms,
the rights and concessions
In the Western medicine the taste is sweet,
the effect soporific.
May God protect us from the fervor of
MPs speeches!
These capitalists' quarrels are there to
extract more money.
You think this colourful, fragrant mirage
is a garden!
Oh You ignorant! You have taken the
cage as your nest![192]

The idea of democracy was the creation of Western thought which British imperial power brought

to India. Iqbal was sceptical about its introduction
in the country as Muslims were in a minority, they
would be left at the mercy of the Hindu majority.
Hindu-Muslim riots during the 1930's made him
apprehensive and he wrote about his concern to E.J.
Thompson[193] in 1934.

> You know I am no believer in democracy. The
> step towards democracy (fatal in my opinion)
> has been taken. We must prepare ourselves for
> financial ruin, the political chaos and despo-
> tism of Hinduism which are likely to follow
> the introduction of democracy in this vast,
> undisciplined and starving country.[194]

Despite this stinging criticism of Western democracy
what Iqbal advocated in his writings was a "spiritual
democracy". This means a democratic government
assimilating the spirit of Islamic teachings. In Islam
sovereignty belongs to Allah. He alone is the Ruler of
the Universe whereas in a democracy the sovereignty
of the people is enshrined. Again in a democracy
preference is given to the opinion of the majority
although a minority may be advocating the path of
truth and righteousness. In Islam the criterion of right
and wrong is not the majority vote but ethical merit.
A democratic vote could exploit people of another
country whereas in Islam one is honour bound to
respect the rights of others. Spiritual democracy is the
vicegerency of man on earth under the sovereignty

of Allah. It gives the supremacy to the Shari'ah in all human affairs. Thus whatever the Parliament legislates must be in the light of the Qur'ān and the Sunnah. Thus, it is bound by Islamic ethical values. It is not like a monster let loose, devastating the cities and fields and causing ruin everywhere.[195]

> Whether it is the majesty of monarchy or
> the spectacle of democracy
> When religion is divorced from politics it
> leads to oppression and tyranny.[196]

Iqbal is not alone in criticizing democracy as many Western plural and social scientists are equally loath-some of this system of government. Important figures associated with anti-democratic thought include Martin Heidegger (1889–1976), Charles Maurras (1868–1952), Friedrich Nietzsche (1844–1900), Carl Schmitt (1888–1985), Oswald Spengler (1880–1936) and others. They maintained that democracy is eco-nomically inefficient, politically unrealistic, dysfunc-tional and morally corrupt. Democracy is also subject to criticism from pro-democratic thought that tends to acknowledge its flaws but stresses a lack of ap-pealing alternatives. In Iqbal's view, Islamic spiritual democracy is a superior political system.

34

Capitalism

The owner of the factory is a useless man
He loves pleasure and shuns hard work.
God decrees: "Man has nothing except
what he strives for."
Why should the capitalist enjoy the fruit
of labour's efforts?[197]

Capitalism is an economic system based upon private ownership of the means of production. In this system the capital is given preference over all other factors in production especially labour. This often leads to the exploitation and abuse of the workers. In this system the wealth is accumulated by a few capitalists and their families to the detrimental consequence of the rest of the humanity. Iqbal had great sympathy for the downtrodden and oppressed section of society as Islam does not tolerate abuse and tyranny instead it has prescribed *zakah* and charity in order to create equality in society and its economic system is geared to promote an egalitarian society. Thus criticism of the capitalist system is evident from Iqbal's writings. This view is well expressed in his poem *Lenin Khudā Kay Ḥuḍūr Mein* (*Lenin in the presence of God*) in which he sympathized with Lenin's complaint before God:

> Europe is ablaze with knowledge and skills
> Truly its fountain of life is in pitch darkness.
> In splendour, in seduction and in grace,
> The buildings of banks outsoar the churches!
> What they call commerce is a game of dice;
> For one, profit, for millions swooping death.
> Their science, philosophy, scholarship, government
> Preach man's equality and drink man's blood.[198]

Iqbal's real concern and sympathies with poor workers, farmers and oppressed human beings was expressed in one of his long poems *Khiḍr-i-Rāh*, where he encountered the wandering Khiḍr.[199] He raised many questions with him about contemporary political and social issues; one of them being the tussle between Capital and Labour. To which Khiḍr replies:

> Give my message to the labouring persons
> It is not only my message but is a universal message.

O whom the fraudulent capitalist has destroyed!
Your destiny hung neglected for centuries.
Those who created the wealth get wages
As the wealthy pay charity to the poor.
The sorcerer of Almūt²⁰⁰ drugged you
with hashish
And O you negligent! Took it like a mint.
Race, nation, church, empire, civilization,
colour
The capitalists concocted these assortments
of intoxicants.
The ignorant sacrificed their life for these
mythical gods.
Losing your life's earnings for the love
of intoxicants.
The deceitful tricks of the capitalists
Checkmated the simple workers.²⁰¹

In Islam wealth and property are *amānah* (trust) from the Creator. Hence human beings are required to spend it lawfully upon themselves, their family and other dependents. On the surplus wealth Allah has created a right for the poor, infirm and deprived. One is morally bound to provide for the downtrodden and deprived section of society. According to Iqbal all natural resources and produce from the earth are there for sharing as it is God Who provides the suitable natural environment for them to grow. Although man makes the efforts to cultivate the land but it is God who brings forth the fruits. Iqbal has depicted this beautifully in his poem *al-Arḍ Lillāh* (*The Earth belongs to Allah*):

> Who cultivates the seed in the darkness
> of the soil?
> Who raises the clouds from the tides of
> the ocean?
> Who brings the favourable wind from
> the West?
> Whose soil is this? Whose is the light
> of the sun?
> Who adorned the wheat on its cobs?
> Who taught the weather its revolutionary
> ways?
> O landlord! This earth is neither yours
> nor mine!
> Nor does it belong to your father or to
> you or to me![202]

The ugly face of capitalism is manifested by creating the craving for wealth and materialism. The multinational companies form cartels and force governments for concessions. They were responsible for the exploitation of poor countries. According to Iqbal capitalism is a system based on abuse and suppression of poor people and nations to fill the treasuries of wealthy capitalists and colonial states. As capitalism is not beneficial to society and does not match with human nature, it is bound to fail sooner or later.

35

Marxism

Farmān-i-Khudā–Farishtun se
(*God's Command to His Angels*)

Rise, and from their slumber wake the poor
ones of My world!
Shake the walls and windows of the
mansions of the great!
Kindle with the fire of faith the blood
of My slaves!
Make the fearful sparrow bold to meet the
falcon's hate!
Close the hour approaches of the kingdom
of the poor–
Every imprint of the past find and annihilate!
Find the field whose harvest is no peasant's
daily bread–
Garner in the furnace every ripening ear
of wheat!
Banish from the house of God the mumbling
priest whose prayers
Like a veil creation from Creator separate!
God by man's prostrations, by man's vows
idols cheated–

Quench at once My shrine and their fane
the sacred light!
Rear for me another temple, build its wall
with mud–
Wearied of their columned marbles, sickened
is My sight!
This fine new world, a workshop filled with
brittle glass–
Go! My poet of the East to madness
dedicate.[203]

*T*he Industrial Revolution during the eighteenth and nineteenth centuries adopted new manufacturing processes. This transition included going from hand production methods to machines. The industries most affected were chemical manufacturing, iron production and textile. These industries attracted many unskilled workers from villages to the factories and mills in cities and towns. They were paid very low wages and their working and living conditions were appalling. This was the disgusting aspect of capitalism. As a reaction to this exploitation of the working class thinkers like Karl Marx (1818–1883) and Friedrich Engels (1820–1895) presented new political and economic theories which later became known as Marxism or Communism. Marxism is the system of socialism in which the dominant feature is public ownership of the means of production, distribution, and exchange. Much impressed by these ideas of Marx, Iqbal has said:

> That Moses without enlightenment and
> Jesus without a cross
> He was no Prophet, yet had a book under
> his arm.[204]

When the Russian Revolution in 1917 took place, which brought the Communists into power, Iqbal who always stood for the rights of the poor, dispossessed and exploited people, hailed it as a new dawn for humanity and wrote:

> A new sun has born from the womb
> of the universe
> How long will you mourn the death
> of stars?[205]

And in his long poem *Saqī Nāmah* he hailed this revolution as:

> The fashions of the age turn round,
> From new-tuned strings new harmonies sound;
> The Frankish wiles have so leaked out
> The Frankish mystagogue halts in doubt,
> The hoary arts of politics sink,
> In earth's nostrils King and Sultan stink,
> The cycle of capitalism is done,
> The juggler has shown his tricks and gone.[206]

Iqbal wrote such poems as *Ishtrākīyat* (*Marxism*) and *Farmān-i-Khudā – Farishtun se* (*God's Command to His Angels*) quoted above hailing the advent of Marxism. His admiration was due to his belief that Communism claimed to provide equal opportunities – political, social and economic to all. As Karl Marx made this slogan "From each according to his ability, to each according to his needs (or need)" in his writings.

Later on Iqbal realized that although proclaiming to stand for the rights of the workers, Communism and its materialistic and agnostic philosophy was anti-religion and was equally harmful for mankind. In practice Communist rule in Russia became the worst dictatorial regime in history. Thus he commented:

> Even if the power is in the hands of workers
> There are the same old tricks of kingship.[207]

Iqbal was disappointed with this turn of events in the Soviet Union under the virtual dictatorship of Lenin and Stalin. He concluded that both Capitalism and Communism are man-made and are equally disastrous for mankind. In Iqbal's view the future for the salvation of mankind lies in Islam as both capitalism and socialism failed to provide a just and equitable system to lead to peace and prosperity. Iqbal constituted an imaginary Consultative Council of the Satan (*Iblīs kī Majlis-i-Shūrā*) and recorded its interesting proceedings about the affairs of the world.

When one of the advisors said that Communism will hinder their work; Satan responds that he does not feel any threat from Communism as it will not guide humanity. However, he is afraid of Islam which still has the capacity to lead the world on to the path of God. Thus Satan observes:

> I have fear from none but from this *ummah*
> Whose burnt out ashes have still a
> smoldering cinder.
> Still there are a few among them we
> can see
> Who perform ablution from their
> dripping tears.
> He knows on whom the future events
> are manifest
> Islam not Communism is the problem
> of the future.[208]

Thus, in Iqbal's view a system based on Divine revelation rather than one devised by man with his limited knowledge is far superior and a blessing for mankind. As both these systems – Capitalism and Marxism – are based on materialism they leave the soul barren. Iqbal's works are replete with this theme.

36

Rūmī

Like Rūmī I gave the prayer-call in the Ka'bah;
And I learnt from him the secret of the soul.
He took up the challenge of days gone by
While I took up the challenge of this age.[209]

*I*t is no poetic exaggeration that like Rūmī who dealt
with the turmoil of the Muslim *ummah* after the
invasion of the Mongol army in the 13th-century,
Iqbal countered the dispirited Muslims during the
colonial period engulfing most of the Muslim world.
Iqbal had great admiration for Rūmī and he consid-
ered him as his spiritual guide. There are numerous
references to Rūmī throughout Iqbal's poetry. He
paid glorious tributes to him and there is no parallel
in literary history where a poet has paid such glow-
ing homage to another. He always referred to him
as a *Murshid* (Guide) and sought advice from him to
solve the knotty problems he came across.

The Master from Rūm, a thinker of pure
disposition,
Unraveled the secrets of Life and Death
for us.[210]

In another poem he paid this tribute:

The Master from Rūm, a guide with
vision,
Leads the caravan of those intoxicated
with ecstasy and love;
Whose status is higher than that of the
Moon and the Sun
So that he uses the galaxy as a rope for
his tent.
His heart is illuminated by the light of
the Qur'ān;
Jamshīd's goblet[211] is humbled before him.
The music from that flute-player of
pure disposition,
Has again stirred up a great storm in me.[212]

Jalāluddīn Muhammad Rūmī was born in Balkh,
Khorasan Central Asia on 30 September 1207. He
was a 13th-century poet, jurist, Islamic scholar,
theologian, and Sufi mystic. Rūmī's influence trans-
cended national borders and ethnic differences and
his legacy is treasured by the entire Muslim *ummah*.
To escape the Mongol menace his family migrated
to Konya where his father Bahāuddīn was appointed

by the Seljuk ruler as a preacher and a teacher. Jalāluddīn completed his education in Aleppo and Damascus in Syria and like his father became a teacher. However, his life completely changed when he met a wandering darwish Shamsuddīn from Tabriz, Rūmī's attachment to gain spiritual satisfaction with Shams resulted in him neglecting his students. This led to jealousy on the part of the students and is thought to be instrumental in the disappearance of Shams without leaving any trace. Shams exercised immense spiritual influence on Rūmī and also brought him great solace and composure. This separation led Rūmī to write a passionate lyrical composition that won the admiration of lovers of poetry all over the world. *Divān-i-Shams Tabrīz* as it is known – is a masterpiece of lyrical composition. But Rūmī's *magnum opus* is the *Mathnawī-i-Ma'navī – the Spiritual Couplets* – which in the Muslim world are esteemed as containing gems of Qur'ānic in the Persian language. Its 33,500 verses relate anecdotes and stories derived from the Qur'ān, Hadith and other Islamic texts to teach lessons in morality. It incorporates gems of Islamic wisdom but primarily focuses on emphasizing inward personal development.

Rūmī had great influence on Iqbal and when he wrote *Asrār-i-Khūdī*, *Rumūz-i-Bikhudi* and *Javed Nāmah* he used the metre of Rūmī's *Mathnawī*. But the greatest tribute which Iqbal paid is to take him as a guide in *Javed Namāh* while journeying through the universe and visiting different planets, just like Dante who took Virgil as a guide in his *Divine Comedy*.

The best example of Iqbal approaching Rūmī for guidance on various issues facing the Muslim *ummah* is in the form of a dialogue between the two. It is recorded in a poem entitled *Pīr wa Murīd* (*The Master and the Disciple*). Iqbal poses the question as an Indian Disciple and the Master Rūmī gives answers to all questions through his own verses. A few of these questions are noted below to illustrate:

THE INDIAN DISCIPLE

> Discerning eyes bleed in pain,
> For faith is ruined by knowledge of
> this age.

RŪMĪ

> Fling it on the body, and knowledge
> becomes a serpent;
> Fling it on the heart, and it becomes
> a friend.

THE INDIAN DISCIPLE

> I have mastered knowledge of the East
> and the West,
> But my soul suffers still in agony.

RŪMĪ

> Treatment by quacks makes you more ill,
> Come to the mother who will nurse you
> to health.

The Indian Disciple

Your words provide sustenance to
the East,
Tell me what ailments kill nations?

Rūmī

Every previous nation that perished
Met destruction for taking stone to
be incense.[213]

Thus from this poetic dialogue Iqbal tried to provide answers to the many problems that humanity faces through the poetry of Rūmī highlighting the relevance of his wisdom in guiding an ailing society.

There is great affinity between the two great masters in their art and thought. Though there is a gap of seven centuries between the two there is a remarkable resemblance and similarity in their approach.

Rumi died on 17 December 1273 in Konya at the age 66 and was buried there. A splendid shrine was erected over his place of burial. His epitaph reads:

When we are dead, seek not our tomb in the earth, but find it in the hearts of men.

37

Goethe

Both Shakespeare and Goethe rethink the Divine
thought of Creation.
There is, however, one important difference
between them. The realist Englishman rethinks the
individual; the Idealist German, the Universal. His
Faust is a seeming individual. Only in reality
he is humanity individualised.[214]

I confess I owe a great deal to Hegel, Goethe,
Mirzā Ghālib, Mirzā 'Abdul Qādir Bedil and
Wordsworth. The first two led me into the "inside"
of things, the third and fourth taught me how to
remain oriental in spirit and express after having
assimilated foreign ideals, and the last saved me
from atheism in my student days.[215]

The person whose works left a lasting effect on Iqbal
was of course Rūmī. However, in the West the person
to whom Iqbal owed a great deal was the German

philosopher Goethe. Even before coming to Europe and studying in Germany Iqbal was acquainted with Goethe's writings and thus paid this tribute to him while composing this elegy in 1901 to Ghalib, the famous nineteenth-century Urdu poet.

> O you are resting in the deserted Delhi
> While your peer is sleeping in the garden
> of Weimer.[216]

Johann Wolfgang von Goethe was born on 28 August 1749 in the famous German city of Frankfurt am Main and died on 22 March 1832 in Weimar and was buried there. He was a great literary figure, writing poetry, plays and, novels and was also a scientist, statesman, theatre director, critic, and amateur artist. He is considered to be the greatest German literary figure of the modern era. Goethe occupies a dominant position also as a philosopher and a pioneer of the Romantic Movement. His *Faust* is Europe's greatest long poem since John Milton's *Paradise Lost* and has been staged as a play. This was Iqbal's favourite book and drew much praise from him.

> Goethe picked up an ordinary legend and filled it with the whole experience of the nine-teenth century – nay the entire experience of human race. Thus transformation of an or-dinary legend into a systematic expression of man's ultimate ideal is nothing short of Divine

workmanship. It is as good as the creation of a beautiful universe out of the chaos of formless matter.[217]

Goethe's other book is the celebrated *West Ostlicher Divan*. During the nineteenth century there was a great movement in Germany of translating books from other languages, not only European languages but oriental languages as well. This interest in Eastern culture led to the translation of *Divān-i-Ḥāfiẓ*. When Goethe read this, he was very appreciative and found affinity with this great work of a genius. Thus, Ḥāfiẓ provided a great stimulus to another creative artist to compose this *Divān*. It is divided into twelve books and appropriately starts with the Hijra – migration of the Prophet (peace be upon him) from Makkah to Medina, perhaps signifying Goethe's flight from the West to the East. The *Divān* also included *Notes and Discussions* which serve as an introduction to the history, religion, culture and literature of the East. Iqbal's attraction to Goethe was due to his positive attitude towards Islam. In the *Divān* Goethe has quoted verses from the Qur'ān, emphasized the Oneness of God and man's duty to submit to Him. He wrote: "If Islam means submission to God. We all live and die in Islam's dominion."

The work of such a consummate literary masterpiece challenged Iqbal and evoked a comparable response in him. As this quote from *Stray Reflections* testifies, Iqbal was overawed by Goethe's intellect.

Our Soul discovers itself when we come into contact with a great mind. It is not until I had realized the Infinitude of Goethe's imagination that I discovered the narrow breadth of my own.[218]

In *Divān* Goethe's restless soul was searching for spiritual bliss and satisfaction from the East. Thus in reply to this Iqbal wrote *Payām-i-Mashriq – Message from the East* to the West. It is significant to note that on the title page Iqbal inscribed: "In response to the *Divān* of the German poet." And in response to Goethe's couplet;

God is of the East possessed
God is Ruler of the West

Iqbal quoted the Qur'ānic verse: "To God belong the East and the West."[219]

In *Payām-i-Mashriq* Iqbal has highlighted the morality and piety in an individual's life. It also touches upon political and social conditions prevalent in India as well as philosophical and literary themes. The section entitled *Mai-i-Bāqī* which is a phrase picked up from one of Ḥāfiẓ's *ghazals* is a tribute to that great poet. It is indeed a great piece of literary work and a befitting reply to Goethe's *Divān*.

38

Nietzsche

That philosopher could not have perceived
the subtlety of *Tawḥīd*
One needs a perceptive vision to unravel
the secrets of *Lā Ilāha*.
His soaring aspiration like an arrow could
pierce the heart of the sky,
His imagination like a scaling ladder could
snare the Sun and the Moon.
Although his recluse life was chaste
Yet he was longing for a taste of sin.[220]

riedrich Nietzsche (1844–1900) was a 19th
century German philosopher whose thought
dominated the West at the time when Iqbal came
to Europe in 1905, just a few years after his death.
Although the nineteenth century was a period
when European power was a dominant force in
the world, Nietzsche's perceptive eyes observed the

hollowness of Western civilization and culture. He was equally unsatisfied with Christianity and other secular ideologies such as democracy, socialism and liberalism. His critique of the Western civilization was a realistic assessment. However, Nietzsche believed there was no spiritual purpose in the Universe. To him there was no ethical principle governing the forces of history. For him virtue, justice and duty as well as love were meaningless terms. He considered that the process of history was determined purely by economic forces and the only principle that governed was 'Might is Right'. One can see the similarity in the approaches of Nietzsche and Marx (1818–1883). Both borrowed this materialistic interpretation of the historical process from the leftwing followers of Hegel (1820–1895) and accepted it without criticism. They, however, drew opposite inferences from this interpretation. Marx predicted that power will eventually fall into the hands of the proletariat by sheer force of historical causes. Nietzsche on the other hand believed that Superman by his might will assert himself. The truth is that these materialistic interpretations of the historical process are flawed.

Nietzsche's philosophy was a perverse reaction against the teachings of Christianity. Thus he purposely opposed the Christian values of magnanimity, humility and asceticism and ascribed egoism, supremacy, despotism and atheism to his concept of Superman.

As Iqbal observed:

> He pierced the heart of the West,
> His hands are crimson with the blood of
> the Church.
> He has built a temple on the foundation
> of the Ka'bah
> His heart is *Mu'min* his intellect is *kāfir*.[221]

The last line alludes to the Prophet's comment about an Arab poet Ummaya ibn Ṣalat.

Iqbal studied Nietzsche's writings and this echoed to him with traces of Islamic teachings as well. At that stage Iqbal was reviewing his thoughts on the decline of the Muslim *ummah*. He generally agreed with Nietzsche's analysis of the decaying West. Whereas Nietzsche was influenced by the philosophy of Zoroaster, an ancient religious reformer of Iran and declared the joyful death of God, Iqbal built up his thoughts on Islamic teachings embodied in the Qur'ān and the Sunnah. Hence despite agreeing with Nietzsche's analysis of the disease inflicting the West, Iqbal did not prescribe the remedy suggested by him. Instead he put forward Islam as the way of salvation for humanity. Thus, addressing Nietzsche directly Iqbal wrote:

> If that *majdhūb*-infatuated European
> was alive today
> Then, Iqbal would have explained to
> him the status of the High One.[222]

By calling him *majdhūb* Iqbal is comparing him with
Manṣūr al-Ḥallāj (858–922), a celebrated Sufi who in
one of his moments of ecstasy uttered, *Anā al-Ḥaq* (I
am the Truth – i.e. God) This led to the accusation of
blasphemy and ultimately his crucifixion in Abbasid
Baghdad. Alluding to this Iqbal wrote:

> Once again this uncrucified Ḥallāj
> Delivered the same old message in a
> new way.
> His language is out-spoken, his ideas
> magnificent.
> The West is torn asunder by the sword of
> his oratory;
> His contemporaries could not appreciate
> The significance of his experience.
> He was a *majdhūb* but was regarded as mad.[223]

Paying posthumous tribute Iqbal acknowledges
Nietzsche's philosophical contribution to exposing
the weaknesses of Western civilization and culture.

Some critics maintain that Iqbal's concept of the
Perfect Man is a copy of Nietzsche's Superman. This
is highly misleading as for Nietzsche God is dead
and Superman has replaced Him, Iqbal's Perfect
Man is indeed a man of faith believing in God and
devoted to Him. Of course there are some similarities
between the Perfect Man and Superman. Yet Iqbal
presented the idea of the Perfect Man in opposition
to the Superman.

39

Vision of Pakistan

The caravan of feeble ants will take the
rose petal for a boat
And in spite of all blasts of waves, it shall
cross the river.
I will take out my worn-out caravan in the
pitch darkness of night.
My sighs will emit sparks and my breath
will produce flames.[224]

These prophetic verses which Iqbal wrote in 1907 were for him divinely inspired insight. He disclosed it to his listeners while addressing the students of Cambridge University during his visit to London to attend the Second Round Table Conference in 1931. This was his vision of the country he wanted to be led by Indian Muslims.[225]

Iqbal was an eminent scholar, a competent lawyer, a distinguished poet as well as a prudent politician.

He excelled in all these fields as an accomplished personality.

He was not just an armchair philosopher detached from the day-to-day happenings around him. His association with the All India Muslim League, a political party for promoting and representing the interests of Muslims, started from his London years. In 1908 he was elected as a member of the Executive Committee of the London Branch of the League. This association was a life-long commitment for Iqbal.

Iqbal together with his law practice also started taking part in the political activities in the Punjab Province. In 1926 he was elected as a member of the Punjab Legislative Council. He actively participated in the affairs of the Province particularly regarding the welfare of Muslims as they were discriminated against in the allocations of revenue for education and social affairs. He was also concerned about the poverty of debt-ridden farmers.

One of the major political catalysts in India was the Khilāfat Movement 1919–1924. It was launched, along with the support of Hindus, for the restoration of Khilāfat in Turkey after the First World War. However, when Kemal Ataturk (1881–1938) finally abolished the Khilāfat in 1924 the movement collapsed and Muslims became very demoralized. After this setback the Muslim League could not make much progress. Muhammad Ali Jinnah (1881–1948) who was playing the leading role in the affairs of the Muslim League got disillusioned by the lack of success and went into voluntary exile in London in 1930. Iqbal became very concerned as the Muslim League became very insignificant and he thought that Jinnah was the best man to salvage the Muslim League and restore some confidence amongst the masses. Thus he persuasively convinced Jinnah to return and lead the Muslim League. Eventually, Jinnah returned and made successful efforts to unite Muslims on one platform.

Iqbal became very close to Jinnah as both attended a series of Round Table Conferences in the early 1930s convened by the British Government in London to resolve the constitutional set up of India. The keynote of Iqbal's politics was securing freedom for India and for Muslims the right to follow their own way of life. Iqbal was apprehensive as Hindus were in the majority in India and under democratic rule Muslims would be under their subjugation. He was strongly opposed to the concept of numerical democracy which would inevitably give Hindus hegemony over the whole country. He was interested in the freedom and advancement of Muslims as well as other minorities and safeguarding their legitimate rights and aspirations while preserving their separate identities.

Iqbal took up the presidency of the Muslim League in 1930 and in that capacity he presided at its annual session held in Allahabad and delivered a momentous and historic oration. In his speech he put forward a scheme for a separate political entity for Muslims.

This is what he proposed:

> I would like to see the Punjab, North-West
> Frontier Province, Sind and Baluchistan into
> a single State – Self-Government within the
> British Empire or without the British Empire.
> The formation of the consolidated North-
> West Indian Muslim State appears to be the
> final destiny of the Muslims, at least of the
> North-West India.[226]

Later writing to Jinnah he further proposed a separate
state of Bengal in Eastern India:

> A separate federation of Muslim Provinces,
> reformed on the lines I have suggested above,
> is the only course by which we can secure a
> peaceful India and save Muslims from the
> domination of non-Muslims. Why should not
> the Muslims of North-West India and Bengal
> be considered as nations entitled to self-
> determination just as other nations in India
> and outside India are?[227]

This was the vision of Iqbal and as Jinnah has faith-
fully acknowledged:

> Although a great poet and philosopher, he
> was no less a practical politician. With his firm
> conviction and faith in the ideals of Islam, he

was one of few who originally thought over the feasibility of carving out of India an Islamic state in the North-West Zones which are historically homelands of the Muslims.[228]

Within seventeen years of Iqbal's proposal Pakistan was created in August 1947.

40

Zindah Rūd

My bold and simple mode of life[229]
Has captured each and every heart;
Though my verses are rough and dull
I lay no claim to poet's art.[230]

The Zindah Rūd is translated as 'living stream of life', a pseudonym Iqbal used for himself in his Persian Mathnawī *Javed Nāmah*. By choosing this name Iqbal was perhaps influenced by Goethe's "Song of Muḥammad" in which he compared the Prophet (peace be upon him) as "a life-giving stream". Iqbal translated this poem in *Payām-i-Mashriq* as *Joye-i-Āb (Stream of Water)*. Hence following the footsteps of the Prophet (peace be upon him) he chose the name Zindah Rūd for his spiritual journey.[231]

Iqbal's personality was multifaceted and enchanting, it influenced all those who came into contact with him. He had a calm and serene composure which impressed everyone who met him. He had a broad outlook on life and his love of aesthetics prevailed through his poetry. Yet he was a private person and did not want to publicize his highly talented faculties. He was a poet but much more than that he was a philosopher par excellence. He felt anguish and heartache seeing the pitiable condition of the *ummah* yet he had traits of ecstasy and revelry. He imparted advice and admonition but also had an educational and reforming influence on society. He portrayed the struggle between reason and love as well as between good and evil, faith and disbelief. These contradictory emotions gave him a charming and fascinating personality.

It is interesting to see his image from the clues he had provided in his poetry. He always tried to belittle his firm convictions and faith and tried to highlight his unconventional views. An imaginary dialogue between a religious scholar and Iqbal in a poem entitled *Zuhd aur Rindī* (*Piety and Revelry*) delightfully records various aspects of his personality. The scholar, who happened to be Iqbal's neighbour, was told that Iqbal was not observant of commandments of Shari‘ah and had leanings towards the Shia sect. Although he prayed in the early morning, he would hold musical evenings as well. He had a spotless character yet he mingled with amorous people. In short, he had contradictory attributes in his personality. Once while meeting him by chance Iqbal confessed that he himself did not know the truth about himself. The poem concludes with this couplet:

Even Iqbal does not know Iqbal
By God this is no joke at all.[232]

Thus in some ways he led others to believe that he
was not that observant of Islamic teachings. Yet his
fervent love for the Prophet (peace be upon him) and
his longing to visit Madinah were well known. His
love and reverence for the Qur'ān is manifested in
his writings. He was observant of *Tahajud* prayers
which he continued even in the bitter and cold nights
of London.

Wintry winds in London were piercing
like swords
Yet I didn't forego the routine of
nightly vigil.[233]

Deprive me not from the blessings of
morning sighs
With your casual loving look, weaken not
your scornful sight.[234]

Iqbal had sufistic leanings and considered himself a
qalandar and *faqīr* (poor and indigent person). This
he had expressed several times in his poetry.

Come to the assembly of Iqbal and drink
a couple of goblets.
Though he does not shave his head, he
knows what *qalandarī* is.

He was aware of his wisdom and penetrating in-
sight. He was fearful as he saw no one taking over
his mantle. He kept hoping and praying for someone
to come along and lead.

> Give to the youth my dawn's sigh
> Give these eaglets wings again.
> O Lord! This is my only wish
> That my insight should be shared by all.[235]

> Endow the young with fervent souls;
> Grant them my vision and my love.[236]

Just months before his death he composed this mel-
ancholy quatrain, lamenting that there is no one to
take his place:

> Will the song of departed age return?
> Will the breeze from Ḥijāz come back?
> The time of this destitute has come
> Will there be another one who knows
> all secrets come?[237]

Endnotes

1. Bāl-i-Jibra' īl 28/320.
2. Ḍarb-i-Kalīm 53/515. Tawhīd means Oneness of God.
3. The Reconstruction of Religious Thought in Islam. Lahore: Shaikh Muhammad Ashraf, 1971 p.64–5.
4. Bāng-i-Darā 98,
5. Bāl-i-Jibra'īl 53–4/ 345–6.
6. Ḍarb-i-Kalīm 34/496.
7. Ibid. 15/477.
8. Bāng-i-Darā 280.
9. Payām-i-Mashriq 114/284.
10. Bāl-i-Jibra'īl 7/299.
11. Javed Nāmah 193/781.Translation by A.J. Arberry.
12. Ibid. 194/782.
13. Bāl-i-Jibra'īl 114/406.
14. Bāl-i-Jibra'īl 132/424.
15. Ibid. 28/320.
16. Bāng-i-Darā 179.
17. A mountain range some distance from Madinah.
18. A plain near Madinah.
19. Bāl-i-Jibra'īl 111/404.
20. Ibid. 122–3/414–5. Translation by V.G. Kiernan.
21. Payām-i-Mashriq 25/195.
22. Darb-i-Kalīm 15/477.
23. Bal-i-Jibra'īl 126/418.
24. Bāng-i-Darā 148.
25. Bāl-i-Jibraīl 93/385.
26. Ibid. 94/386.
27. Bāng-i-Darā p. 259.
28. Bāl-i-Jibra'īl 86/378.
29. The Reconstruction of Religious Thought in Islam. p.34.
30. Ibid. p.65.

31. Be and it becomes is the Qur'ānic expression kun fayakūn. This refers to the act of creation and the power of God. When God says: "Kun–Be" and it instantly happens.

32. Allusion is to the tragic story of Farhād who had to dig into a mountain base conveying a stream to win over his beloved Shirīn.

33. Bāng-i-Darā 258–9.

34. Bāl-i-Jibra'īl 128/420.

35. Payām-i-Mashriq 166/336.

36. Bāng-i-Darā 155.

37. Ibid. 157.

38. Bāng-i-Darā 229–30.

39. Ibid. 254.

40. Bāl-i-Jibra'īl 126–7. Translation by Naim Siddiqui.

41. Zubūr-i-'Ajam p.116/508

42. Bāng-i-Darā 233–4.

43. Zubūr-i-'Ajam 84

44. Khidr is supposed to be given special knowledge from God and guided the Prophet Mūsā (peace be upon him) revealing the mysteries of Divine purpose behind events happening in the world. He is endowed with eternal life.

45. He is Elijah of the Old Testament and is expected to come back along with Khidr during the Last Judgement. He is also supposed to possess supernatural powers.

46. Bāl-i-Jibra'īl 144/436.Translation by Mustansir Mir.

47. Ibid. 15/657

48. Darb-i-Kalīm 146/608.

49. Chosen One is the translation of Mustafa being one of the names of the Prophet (peace be upon him), while Abū Lahab was his uncle but an arch enemy.

50. Bāng-i-Darā p. 223.

51. Ibid. p. 274.

52. Javed Nāmah 137–8/725–6.

53. Payām-i-Mashriq 53/223.

54. Darb-i-Kalīm 16/478.

55. Payām-i-Mashriq 192/362

56. Bāl-i-Jibra'īl 129/421. Translation by V.G. Kiernam.

57. Darb-i-Kalīm 64/526.

58. Bāng-i-Darā 278.

59. Bāl-i-Jibra'īl 84/376.
60. Ḍarb-i-Kalīm 20–1/482–3.
61. Bāl-i-Jibra'īl 43/335. Translation by Syed Akbar Ali Shah.
62. Ibid. 67/359.
63. Jāvaid Nāmah 81/669.
64. Rumūz-i-Bikhudi 121–3.
65. Bāl-i-Jibra'īl 78/370.
66. Ḍarb-i-Kalīm 35/497.
67. Bāl-Jibra'īl 25/317.
68. Ibid. 38/330.
69. Ibid. 40/332.
70. Iqbal gifted this quatrain to one of his admirers Muhammad Ramzan 'Ata'ī at his request. However, there is a similar quatrain in Armaghān-i-Ḥijāz.
71. Bāng-i-Darā 208.
72. Rumūz-i-Bikhudi 170.
73. Ḍarb-i-Kalīm 44/506.
74. Bāng-i-Darā 271.
75. Ḍarb-i-Kalīm 60/522
76. Ibid.
77. Sūrah al-Baqarah 2: 28.
78. Bāl-i-Jibra'īl 165/457.
79. Ibid. 156/448.
80. https://www.thesufi.com/5–characteristsic-allama-iqbals-shaheen-mascot-khudi/
81. Ibid. 38/330.
82. Ibid. 120/412.
83. Ibid. 14/306.
84. Ibid. 17/309.
85. Ibid. 116/408.
86. Ibid. 46/38.
87. Ibid. 61/353.
88. Ḍarb-i-Kalīm 72/534.
89. Bāng-i-Darā 174.
90. Ḍarb-i-Kalīm 48/510.
91. Bāng-i-Darā 265.
92. Ḍarb-i-Kalīm 58/520.
93. Bāng-i-Darā 160.
94. Ibid. 161,
95. Ibid. 273.

96. Ibid. 270.
97. Iqbal Nāmah vol.2 letter no. 59.
98. Bāng-i-Darā 203.
99. Ibid. 203–4.
100. Ibid. 202.
101. Ibid. 201.
102. Armaghān-i-Ḥijāz Urdu 38/680.
103. Quoted in Ghulam Rasul Malik: Surūd-i-Saḥr Āfrīn. Lahore: Iqbal Academy Pakistan, 2007. p.45.
104. The Reconstruction of Religious Thought in Islam. p.124.
105. Bāl-i-Jibra'īl 166/458. Translation by V.G. Kiernan
106. Ibid. 73/365.
107. Bāng-i-Darā 248–9.
108. Rumūz-i-Bikhudi 85–6.
109. Bāng-i-Darā 190.
110. Stray Reflections p.88.
111. Bāng-i-Darā 174.
112. Lectures on the Reconstruction of Religious Thought in Islam. p. 131.
113. Rumūz-e-Bikhudi 125.
114. Lectures on the Reconstruction of Religious Thought in Islam. 138.
115. Ḍarb-i-Kalīm 15/477.
116. Bāl-i-Jibra'īl 127/419.
117. Asrār-i-Khūḍī 18.
118. Syed Abdul Vahid: Thoughts and Reflections of Iqbal. Lahore: Muhammad Ashraf, 1964. p. 244.
119. Sūrah al-Fajr 89:27.
120. Bāl-i-Jibra'īl 55/347.
121. Rumūz-i-Bikhudi 94.
122. Sūrah al-Zumar 39:53.
123. Sūrah al-Ra'd 13:11.
124. Rumūz-i-Bikhūdī 85.
125. Bāng-i-Darā 190.
126. Rumūz-i-Bikhūdī 86.
127. Rumūz-i-Bikhudi 155.
128. Bāl-i-Jibra'īl 160/ 452.
129. M. Fethullah Gulen: Key Concepts in the Practice of Sufism Izmir: Kaynak, n.d. p.198.

130. "Faqr is my pride" is a Hadith which some scholar consider as da'īf (weak).

131. This is the second hemistich of a verse of Ḥāfiz Shīrāzī. The first reads as: The beauty of the beloved does not need our incomplete love.

132. Bāng-i-Dara 180.

133. Armaghān-i-Ḥijāz Urdu 48/690.

134. Bāl-i-Jibra'īl 59/351.

135. Bāng-i-Dara 269–273.

136. Bāl-i-Jibra'īl 81/373.

137. Ḍarb-i-Kalīm 82/544.

138. Dars-i-Nizami is a study curriculum used in traditional Islamic institutions (madrasahs) and Dār al-'Ulūms, which originated in the Indian subcontinent in the 19th century. It was designed by Mullā Nizām Uddīn Al-Sihalwi (d.1748).

139. Maktab is an elementary school usually attached to a mosque.

140. Ibid. 79/541.

141. Bāl-i-Jibra'īl 32/324.

142. Ibid. 46/338.

143. Ḍarb-i-Kalīm 58/520.

144. Bāng-i-Dara 209.

145. Bāng-i-Dara 284.

146. In Sufi terminology Saqī (literary means a cup-bearer) is one who serves the wine of God's love.

147. Bāl-i-Jibra'īl 12/304.

148. Payām-Mashriq 98/268.

149. Bāl-i-Jibra'īl 83/375.

150. Ḍarb-i-Kalīm 111/573.

151. Iqbal used the word Ibrāhīm, referring to the Prophet Ibrāhīm's (peace be upon him) smashing of idols.

152. Ḍarb-i-Kalīm 26/488.

153. Ḍarb-i-Kalīm 118–9/580–1.

154. Bāl-i-Jibra'īl 95,101/387–393.Translation by Saleem A. Gilani with some modifications.

155. Ḍarb-i-Kalīm 105/567.

156. Ibid. 129/591.

157. Ḍarb-i-Kalīm 94/556.

158. Plato (428–348 BC) was a Greek philosopher and the founder of the Academy in Athens, the first institution of higher learning in the Western world.
159. Darb-i-Kalīm 92/554.
160. Darb-i-Kalīm 96/558.
161. Rumūz-i-Bikhudī 150–1.
162. Rumūz-i-Bikhūdī 153.
163. Ibid. 153.
164. Bāl-i-Jibra'īl 154/446.
165. Ibid. 119–120/ 411–12.
166. Bāng-i-Darā 180.
167. Javed Nāmah 206–7/794–5.
168. Ibid. 208/796.
169. Bāl-i-Jibra'īl 63/355.
170. Bāng-i-Darā 34. Translation by M.A.K. Khalil with some modifications.
171. Ibid. 83.
172. Ibid. 31.
173. Bāng-i-Darā 141.
174. Asrār-i-Khūdī 76.
175. Bāl-i-Jibra'il 24/316.
176. Man of Faith.
177. Refers to a Hadith, in which Allah informed the Prophet, peace be upon him: 'Were it not for you, I would not have created the Universe. (law laka lamā khalaqtu'l-aflāk).'Some consider this Hadith to be a forged one.
178. Bāl-i-Jibrīl p.66–7/358–9.
179. Bāl-i-Jibra'īl 40/332.
180. It means that those who rule the body and those who rule the soul are united in one personality. Junayd of Baghdad (835–910) was a Persian mystic and one of the most famous Sufis. Ardashir (180–242 AD), was the founder of the Sasanian Empire in Persia.
181. Bāl-i-Jibra'īl 118/410. Translated by Naim Siddiqi except last four lines which were provided by the author.
182. Bāng-i-Darā 261.
183. Darb-i-Kalīm 152–3/614–5.

- A TREASURY OF IQBAL -

184. Bāng-i-Darā 160.
185. Bang-i-Dara 159.
186. Ibid. 267.
187. Ibid. 248.
188. B.A. Dar: Letters and Writings of Iqbal.
189. Bāng-i-Darā 265.
190. Ḍarb-i-Kalīm 149/611.
191. Payām-i-Mashriqı35/305.
192. Bāng-i-Darā 261.
193. Edward John Thompson (1886–1946) was a British scholar, novelist and historian. He was a keen observer of Indian politics and was sympathetic to the aspirations of the Indian nationalists.
194. S. Hasan Ahmad: The Idea of Pakistan and Iqbal: A disclaimer. Patna; Khuda Buksh Oriental Public Library, 2003. p. 88.
195. Zubūr-i-'Ajam 167/559.
196. Bāl-i-Jibra'īl 40/332.
197. Bāng-i-Darā 291.
198. Bāl-i-Jibra'īl 107/399.
199. Khiḍr or al-Khiḍr is a figure ascribed to a person in the Qur'ān as a righteous servant of God possessing great wisdom or mystic knowledge to which the Prophet Mūsā was sent to acquire knowledge as mentioned in Sūrah al-Kahf.
200. Almūṭ was the secret fortress of the assassins.
201. Bāng-i-Darā 262–3.
202. Bāl-i-Jibra'īl 119/411.
203. Bāl-i-Jibra'īl 109–10/401–2. Translation by V. G. Keirnan.
204. Armaghān-i-Ḥijāz Urdu 8/650.
205. Bāng-i-Darā 263.
206. Bāl-i-Jibra'īl 123/415.
207. Ibid. 40/332.
208. Armaghān-i-Ḥijāz Urdu 12/654.
209. Armaghān-i-Ḥijāz, Farsi 56/938.
210. Payām-i-Mashriq 30/190.
211. A goblet in which Jamshīd, an ancient Iranian King could see whatever he wished.
212. Pas Che Bāyad Kard ae Aqwām-i-Sharq 7/803.
213. Bāl-i-Jibra'īl 134–5, 7/426, 7, 9.

214. Stray Reflections p. 130.
215. Ibid. p.53.
216. Bāng-i-Dārā 26.
217. Stray Reflections. p. 66.
218. Ibid. p.16.
219. al-Baqarah 2: 142.
220. Ḍarb-i-Kalim 83–4/545–6.
221. Piyām-i-Mashriq p. 201
222. Bāl-i-Jibra'īl 56/348.
223. Javed Nāmah 152/740.
224. Bāng-i-Dārā 141–2.
225. Iqbal's contribution to Literature & Politics. Lahore: Iqbal Academy, n.d. pp. 12–3.
226. Presidential Address at the All India Muslim League, Allahabad Session December 1930.
227. Letter of 21st June 1937 to Quaid-i-Azam Muhammad Ali Jinnah.
228. Evolution of Pakistan p. 121 quoted by Syed Abdul Vahid in Studies in Iqbal. Lahore: Muhammad Ashraf, 1967.
229. The word used by Iqbal is Qalandarī which difficult to translate. In Sufism this is a term used for those who abandon the worldly goods and wander around. He has also used the word faqīr in the same sense.
230. Bāl-i-Jibra'īl 48/340. Translation by Syed Akbar Ali Shah.
231. Javed Iqbal: Zindah Rūd. Lahore: Sheikh Ghulam Ali, 1979. vol. 1 p. iv.
232. Bāng-i-Dārā 60.
233. Bāl-i-Jibra'īl 40/332.
234. Ibid. 16/308.
235. Bāl-i-Jibra'īl 86/378.
236. Ibid. 124/416.
237. Armughān-i-Ḥijāz, Persian 12/894.

Glossary of Terms

ʿAql	Reason, intellect.
Band'-i-Ṣaḥraḥī	Wandering person.
Bikhūdī	Selflessness, State of Obliviousness
Chirāg-i-rāh	Lamp for indicating the path.
Dars-i-Nizāmī	*Dars-i-Nizāmī* is a study curriculum used in traditional Islamic institutions (madrasahs) and Dār al-ʿUlūms, which originated in the Indian subcontinent in the 19th century. It was designed by Mullā Nizām Uddīn Al-Sihalwī (d. 1748).
Darwish	Indigent, destitute, free of worldly needs.
Dīn	Religion, system of beliefs and way of life.
Faqr	*Faqr* is usually translated as poverty, but for Iqbal it represents self-sufficiency and contentment.
Faqir	This comes from the same root as *faqr* and often translated as beggar but Iqbal used it to mean contended.
Fiqh	Islamic law and jurisprudence.
Fuquhā'	(sing. *faqīh*) Jurists.
Ghaffār	One of the attributes of God meaning Forgiving.
Ghazal	Ode, the most popular form of poetry in Persian and Urdu. It contains a minimum of five couplets in which there is

no continuity of subject and each couplet deals with a different topic. Each couplet rhymes and has the same metre. Love compositions.

Ḥadīth	A saying and action of the Prophet as well as his tacit approval by his silence on acts performed in his presence. Its plural is *aḥādīth*.
Ijmāᶜ	Consensus of opinion of jurists.
Ijtihād	Juristic reasoning by a suitably qualified scholar of Islamic jurisprudence based on Islamic legal sources.
ᶜIlm	Knowledge.
ᶜIshq	Intense or passionate love.
Īmān	Belief, faith.
Jabarūt	Omnipotence, power, might.
Jannah	Garden – the term usually used in the Qur'an to refer to Paradise.
Jibrīl	The archangel Gabriel.
Jihād	Struggle, Resistance against evil.
Kāfir	From *kufr* whose literal meaning is to cover up. One who covers up or denies God's existence. Thus, it is the opposite of faith (*īmān*) and the one who does not accept the tenets of Islam. It is often translated as infidel. In Iqbal's poetry it is not often used in its theological meaning, but signifies lack of faith and the burning zeal of *īmān* identified as love of God.
Khalīfah	Vicegerent. The purpose of Adam's creation was to send him and his wife as vicegerents on Earth.

Khilāfah	Caliphate.
Khidr	According to authentic traditions, he is the person who guided the Prophet Musa (peace be upon him) in the story mentioned in Surah al-Kahf (18: 65–82). He is considered a righteous servant of God possessing great wisdom or mystic knowledge and aids those in distress. He acts as a spiritual guide and is immortal living near rivers and seas and helps travellers.
Khirad	Reason, wisdom.
Khudā	The One God, Creator of the universe. It is a Persian word.
Khūdī	The Ego, I, Self. Iqbal has used it meaning self-assertion, self-realization or self-respect.
Lā ilāha illā Allāh	First part of the Article of Faith stating "There is no deity except God." The second part being: "Muḥammad is His Messenger".
Majdhūb	One who is lost in contemplation and thus is not in full possession of his senses. One of the stages in the life of a mystic when he is overwhelmed by the radiation of Divine Presence.
Madrasah	Simply means the same as school does in the English language, whether that is private, public or parochial school, as well as for any primary or secondary school.
Maktab	Elementary *madrasah*.
Maʿrifah	Knowledge of God.

Miʿrāj	The ascension of the Prophet (peace be upon him) to Heaven. In the first stage of the night journey the Prophet was taken to Jerusalem and then continued his flight to the heavens.
Millat	Nation. It is used as a synonym of *ummah*. A community based on religion hence used for Muslims.
Mathnawī	*Mathnawī* is derived from *mathnā* meaning two. In poetry it means a poem in which each couplet's *miṣraʿ* (line of a verse, hemistich) rhymes. However each couplet has a different rhyme. There is no limitation on the number of couplets, but the theme should remain the same and so also the metre. This form of poetry is particularly used for descriptions of battles and romances. In Persian, besides Rūmī's *Mathnavi* Firdusī's *Shāhnāmah* is a very well known *mathnavī*.
Mujāhid	Warrior. In Islamic terminology one who struggles in the path of Allah.
Mu'min	A person of faith, a believer. *Mu'min* and Muslim are used interchangeably. However, Muslim means one who submits to the will of God. Thus *Mu'min* refers to belief and Muslim to one who practices their faith.
Mushāʿarah	A gathering for the recital of poetry. It is a popular social and literary event in India and Pakistan.
Nafs	Soul, spirit, self.

Nafs al-muṭma'innah	A happy, peaceful and satisfied soul living in obedience to Allah.
Nūr	Light.
Qahhār	One of the attributes of God denoting to His absolute power.
Qalandar	In Sufism this term is used for those who abandon the worldly needs and wander around. Iqbal has also used the word *faqīr* in the same sense
Qiyās	Analogical deduction or basing legal ruling on a similar case.
Quddūs	One of the attributes of God, meaning Most Holy.
Risālah	Message, Messengership.
Shāhīn	Royal white falcon, a bird of prey. Iqbal has used other species such as 'uqab (eagle) and baz (hawk) as well.
Sajjadah Nashīn	Keeper of the tombs of saints.
Sharī'ah	The Islamic legal code which embraces all aspects of life.
Shaytān	Satan or the Devil. Iblis is his proper name used in the Qur'ān.
Sunnah	The practice of the Prophet.
Taqlid	Following, imitation. Refers to those jurists who follow the rulings laid down by earlier *fuquhā'* instead of using *ijtihād*.
Taṣawwuf	Islamic mysticism not influenced by other schools of Sufism.
Tawḥīd	The Oneness of God. One the most essential beliefs of Muslims.
'Ulamā'	(sing. *'alim*) Scholars of religious sciences.

Ummah	Muslim Community, Nation. Sometimes the word *millat* is used for *ummah*.
Ustad	A Teacher or a mentor.
Waḥdat al-Wujūd	Doctrine propounded by Ibn al-ʿArabī that only existence in the universe is of God other things being just shadows.
Zakāh	Its literal meaning is purification. One of the Pillars of Islam whereby Muslims are required to spend in charitable causes two and a half per cent of their savings every year.

Bibliography

The Bibliography consists of the following parts:

a. The works of Iqbal in chronological order of publication and with translations (those that are available in English.

b. Collected Works and Selections

c. A select list of a few important biographies and critical appreciations of Iqbal's works mainly in English but includes some significant books in Urdu as well.

(a) Works of Iqbal

1. The Development of Metaphysics in Persia. (Thesis, Munich). (Cambridge: Cambridge University Press, 1908).

2. Asrār-i-Khūdī (Persian). (Lahore: Hakim Faqir Mohammed Chishti Nizami,1915).
   Reynold A. Nicholson: The Secrets of the Self (Asrār-i-Khūdī): A Philosophical Poem. (London: Macmillan, 1920).

3. Rumūz-i-Bikhudi (Persian). (Lahore: Hakim Faqir Mohammed Chishti, 1918).
   A.J. Arberry: The Mystery of Selflessness (verse translation). (London: J. Murray, 1953).

4. Payām-i-Mashriq (Persian) (Delhi: Maṭbaʿ Jamia Milliay Islamiya, 1923).

R. A. Nicholson: *The Message of the East.* (Islamica I. 1925).

5. Bāng-i-Darā (Urdu). (Lahore, 1924).
   M. A. K. Khalil: Call of the Marching Bell (verse translation). (Lahore, 1997).

6. Zubūr-i-'Ajam (Persian) (Lahore, 1927).
   A.J. Arberry: Persian Psalms (verse translation). (Lahore: Muhammad Ashraf, 1948).

7. Six Lectures on the Reconstruction of Religious Thought in Islam. (Lahore, 1930).

8. Javed-Nāmah (Persian). (Lahore, 1932).
   J. Arberry: Javed-Nāmah. (London: Allen & Unwin, 1966).

9. Pas Cheh Bāyad Kard Ay Aqwām-i-Sharq (Persian) (Lahore: Kutb Khana Tulu'-i-Islam, 1936). Sheikh Hassan Din: Pas Cheh Bāyad Kard – Then what should be the strategy...? (Lahore: Sheikh Ghulam Ali. 1988).

10. Musāfir (Persian) (Lahore, 1936).
    Maqbool Elahi: Musāfir Mathnawī (A Few Days' Travel in Afghanistan, October 1933). Lahore: Sheikh Ghulam Ali, 1988. [It is bound with Pas Cheh Bāyad Kurd}

11. Bāl-i- Jibra'īl (Urdu) (Lahore: Taj Co., 1935), Naim Siddiqui: Iqbal: Bāl-i-Jibra'īl (a verse translation). (Freemount, California: Alhamra Publications, 1996).

12. Ḍarb-i-Kalīm (Urdu) (Lahore, 1936).
    Syed Akbar Ali Shah: The Rod of Moses. (Lahore: Iqbal Academy, 1983).

13. Armāghān-i-Ḥijāz (Persian and Urdu). (Lahore, 1938).

14. Stray Reflections; edited by Javed Iqbal. (Lahore: Iqbal Academy Pakistan, 1961).

(b) Collected Works and Selections

1. Kullīyyāt-i-Iqbāl – Fārsī (Collected Poetical Works of Iqbal-Persian). (Lahore: Sheikh Ghulam Ali, 1973 repr. 1990).
2. Kullīyyāt-i-Iqbāl – Urdu (Collected Poetical Works of Iqbal – Urdu. (Aligarh: Educational Book House, 1975).
3. Iqbal: A selection of the Urdu Verse: Text and Translation by D.J. Matthews. (London: University of London. School of Oriental and African Studies, 1993).
4. Poems from Iqbal: renderings in English verse with comparative Urdu text; translated by V.G. Kiernan. London: (John Murray, 2nd ed. 1955).
5. Tulip in the Desert: A Selection of the Poetry of Mohammad Iqbal; by Mustansir Mir. London: Hurst, 2000.

(c) General Works on Iqbal

Muhammad Sharif Baqa: Mauḍu'āt-i-Khuṭubāt-i-Iqbal. (Lahore: Iqbal Academy Pakistan, 2007).

Bashir Ahmad Dar: A Study in Iqbal's Philosophy. (Lahore: Sheikh Muhammad Ashraf, 1944).

Khalifa Abdul Hakim: Fikr-i-Iqbal [Urdu] Lahore: Bazm-i-Iqbal, 1957 repr. 1988.

Rafi' al-Din Hashmi, Muhammad Suhail 'Umar [and] Wahid 'Ishrat: Iqbālīyāt ke Sau Sāl. (Lahore: Iqbal Academy Pakistan, 2002)

Rafi' al-Din Hashmi: Kitābīāt-i-Iqbāl [A Bibliography of Iqbal]. (Lahore: Iqbal Academy Pakistan 1977).

Riffat Hassan: The Sword and the Sceptre. (Lahore: Iqbal Academy Pakistan, 1977).

Javed Iqbal: Zindah-Rūd. (The Living Stream – biography in Urdu) (Lahore: Sheikh Ghulam Ali, 1989). 3 vols.

Muhammad Iqbal: The Poet's Vision and Magic of Words: An approach to Iqbal's Poetry. (Lahore: Islamic Book Service, 1978).

Syed Latif Hussain Kazmi: Philosophy of Iqbal. (New Delhi: A.P.H. Publishing Corporation, 1997).

Yusuf Husain Khan: Rūḥ-i-Iqbāl [Urdu].(Lahore: Al-Qamar Enterprises, repr. 1996. First published 1942 in Hyderabad, Deccan.)

Ghulam Rasul Malik: Sarūd-i-Saḥr Āfrīn. Lahore: Iqbal Academy Pakistan, 2007).

Hafeez Malik (ed.): Iqbal: poet-philosopher of Pakistan. (New York: Columbia University Press, 1971). [contains Selected Bibliography pp. 416–429].

Mustansir Mir: Iqbal (London: I.B. Tauris for Oxford Centre for Islamic Studies, 2006).

Abul Hasan Ali Nadvi: Glory of Iqbal [translated from Arabic] by Mohammed Asif Qidwai. (Lucknow: Islamic Research Publications, 1973).

Muhammad Rafiuddin: Ḥikmat-i-Iqbal. (Islamabad: Idarah Tahqiqat-i-Islami, 2006)

Khawja Abdur Rahim (ed.): Iqbal: the Poet of Tomorrow. (Lahore: Ferozsons, 1968).

Annemarie Schimmel: Gabriel's Wing: a Study into the Religious Ideas of Sir Muhammad Iqbal. (Leiden: Brill, 1963). [contains extensive Bibliography pp.388–414]

Abdul Qadir Sheikh: Iqbal: the Great Poet of Islam. (Sang-i-Meal Publications, 1975).

Saeed Shaikh (ed.): Studies in Iqbal's Thought and Art (Select Articles from the Quarterly 'Iqbal'). (Lahore: Bazm-i-Iqbal, 1972).

Abdur Rashid Siddiqui: Man and Destiny: Some Reflections on Iqbal's Concepts of *Khudī* and the Perfect Man (Markfield, Leics.: The Islamic Foundation, 2008).

Syed Abdul Vahid: Glimpses of Iqbal: (Karachi: Iqbal Academy, 1974).

————— Introduction to Iqbal. (Karachi: Maṭbūʻāt-i-Pakistan, 1954)

————— Iqbal: His Art and Thought. (Oxford: Oxford University Press 1969).

————— Studies in Iqbal. (Lahore: Sheikh Muhammad Ashraf, 1967).

————— Thoughts & Reflections of Iqbal. (Lahore: Sheikh Muhammad Ashraf, 1964).

————— ☙◉◐ —————

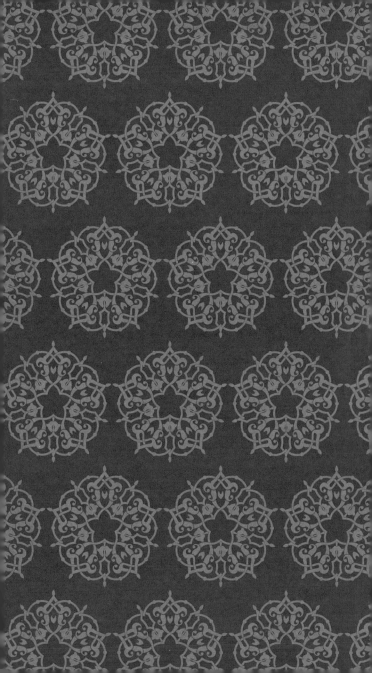